D1710745

Elizabethan World

Almanac

Elizabethan World

Almanac

Sonia G. Benson
Jennifer York Stock, Project Editor

U.X.L
A part of Gale, Cengage Learning

GALE
CENGAGE Learning·

Detroit • New York • San Francisco • New Haven, Conn • Waterville, Maine • London

GALE
CENGAGE Learning

Elizabethan World: Almanac

Sonia G. Benson

Project Editor
Jennifer York Stock

Editorial
Kate Potthoff

Rights and Acquisitions
Margaret Chamberlain-Gaston,
Lisa Kincade

Imaging and Multimedia
Lezlie Light, Michael Logusz, Christine
O'Bryan, Kelly Quin

Product Design
Pamela Galbreath, Jennifer Wahi

Composition
Evi Seoud

Manufacturing
Rita Wimberley

LIBRARY OF CONGRESS CATALOGING-IN-PUBLICATION DATA

Benson, Sonia G.
  Elizabethan world : almanac / Sonia G. Benson ; Jennifer York Stock, project editor.
    p. cm. — (Elizabethan world reference library)
  Includes bibliographical references and index.
  ISBN 13: 978-1-4144-0189-8 (hardcover : alk. paper)
  ISBN 10: 1-4144-0189-2 (hardcover : alk. paper)
  ISBN 13: 978-1-4144-0188-1 (reference library set : alk. paper)
  ISBN 10: 1-4144-0188-4 (reference library set : alk. paper)
  1. Great Britain–History–Elizabeth, 1558-1603–Juvenile literature. 2. Great Britain–Social life
and customs–16th century–Juvenile literature. 3. Great Britain–Civilization–16th century–
Juvenile literature. I. Stock, Jennifer York, 1974– II. Title.
  DA355.B457 2006
  942.05'5–dc22   2006019216

This title is also available as an e-book.
ISBN 13: 978-1-4144-1038-8 (set), ISBN 10: 1-4144-1038-7 (set)
Contact your Gale sales representative for ordering information.

Printed in the United States of America
3 4 5 6 7 8 14 13 12 11 10 09 08

Table of Contents

Reader's Guide

When Elizabeth I (1533–1603) was crowned queen in 1558, England was, compared to other European nations, a poor and backward country. At this time England was deeply divided by religious strife. It was too weak to protect itself from its enemies, lacking a strong military. Furthermore, England had been too beleaguered by its conflicts to participate in the Renaissance, the great artistic and intellectual movement that had swept Europe beginning in the fourteenth century. The people of England must have wondered what the inexperienced twenty-five-year-old queen could possibly do to strengthen her nation.

Nonetheless, when people today think of the Elizabethan Era most envision the dazzling, red-headed queen skillfully reigning over a vibrant court lively with music and dance, splendid costumes, and dashing young statesmen, explorers, and artists. Soon after she took the throne, Elizabeth's moderate religious settlement eased some of the divisions between Protestants and Catholics that had been tearing the nation apart, providing England with a stability that allowed it to grow in many directions. During Elizabeth's reign commerce flourished. London became one of Europe's largest and greatest cities. The era produced unparalleled advances drama, and not surprisingly, the Elizabethan Era has become known as the age of Shakespeare in honor of its leading dramatist and poet. There was growth in other spheres as well. As the new middle class developed, public education advanced, and England experienced a higher level of literacy than ever before. This made it possible for people who were not born into the nobility to rise in position. Elizabeth's reign also marked the beginning of English exploration of the New World. Militarily, Elizabethans restored England to its place as a major European power. When the Spanish Armada arrived in the English Channel in 1588 hoping to invade England, Elizabeth's small but highly skilled navy was up to the task of defending the small island from the world's largest power. The English people celebrated the victory with a new sense of pride in their nationality.

Historians differ greatly over how much credit to give Elizabeth for all the advances that occurred during her reign. Many elements of change were clearly already in process. Although we will probably never determine the extent of her contribution, her story has nevertheless fascinated historians worldwide for centuries after her death. The story of Elizabethan England provides valuable insight not only into English history, but also into the transition of Western society into modern times.

Coverage and features

Elizabethan World: Almanac presents an overview of this golden age of English history and the remarkable cultural, political, religious, and economic developments that occurred during the era. The volume's twelve chapters briefly examine the Tudor monarchy prior to Elizabeth, especially the difficult path from Catholicism to Protestantism beginning in the reign of Elizabeth's father, Henry VIII, and the tumultuous short reigns of her half brother, the Protestant Edward VI, and half-sister, the Catholic Mary Tudor. The achievements of Queen Elizabeth and her talented group of statesmen, such as William Cecil, Robert Dudley, and Francis Walsingham, are presented, including the religious settlement of 1559 and the conflicts with Scotland, Ireland, and Spain. Elizabeth's conflict with Catholics of England and Europe, and some of the conspiracies to overthrow her rule, are also featured. In addition, the *Almanac* places significant emphasis on the culture of the times, from Elizabeth's court to the rural pageants, and from the New World explorations to the remarkable flowering of literature and drama for which the era is renowned. Finally, the volume presents a look at Elizabethan daily life, social structures, holidays, and much more. The volume includes 56 photographs and illustrations, a timeline, a glossary, research and activity ideas, and sources for further reading.

U•X•L Elizabethan World Reference Library

Elizabethan World: Biographies profiles twenty-six significant figures who participated in the transformation of England during the Elizabethan Era. Included are some of Elizabeth's favorites, the statesmen to whom she gave great powers and advantages and who helped her run her country, such as Robert Dudley and Robert Devereux; the sea traders and explorers who opened up the New World and other trade routes, including John Hawkins, Francis Drake, and Walter Raleigh; the scientists, philosophers, and educators who brought England's medieval thinking to new, non-religious inquiry, such as Francis Bacon, Richard Hakluyt, and John Dee. Also featured are the royal opponents of the queen, such as Mary Stuart, Queen of Scots, and King Philip II of Spain; Catholic and Protestant leaders like William Allen and John Knox; and the great writers of the day, including Christopher Marlowe, Philip Sidney, and William Shakespeare. The volume includes 50 photographs and illustrations, a timeline, and sources for further reading.

Elizabethan World: Primary Sources presents eighteen full or excerpted written works, speeches, and other documents that were influential during the Elizabethan Era. Included are speeches and a poem by Elizabeth I; the Catholic pope's bull of 1570 directed against the English queen; and an excerpt from the sensational and highly influential *Book of Martyrs* by John Foxe. Several examples of the literature and journals of the times are featured, including memoirs from the ill-fated settlement in Roanoke, Virginia; an excerpt from Edmund Spenser's *Faerie Queene*, a Shakespeare play and two of his sonnets, and much more. 47 photographs and illustrations, sources for further reading, a timeline, and a list of sources for further reading supplement the volume.

A cumulative index of all three volumes in the U•X•L Elizabethan World Reference Library is also available.

Comments and suggestions

We welcome your comments on *Elizabethan World: Almanac* and suggestions for other topics to consider. Please write: Editors, *Elizabethan World: Almanac*, U•X•L, 27500 Drake Rd. Farmington Hills, Michigan 48331-3535; call toll free: 1-800-877-4253; fax to 248-699-8097; or send e-mail via http://www.gale.com.

Timeline of Events

1494 The Treaty of Tordesillas divides the New World between Spain and Portugal.

1509 Henry VIII takes the English throne.

1512 Nicholaus Copernicus explains his heliocentric theory.

October 31, 1517 German monk Martin Luther nails to a church door his list of ninety-five statements attacking certain Roman Catholic practices.

1520s The Protestant Reformation movement sweeps through major parts of Europe.

1530s The Catholic Church refuses to grant Henry VIII a divorce from his first wife. Henry breaks with the church, declares himself head of the church in England, and marries Anne Bolelyn.

1536 John Calvin sets up his Protestant government in Geneva, Switzerland.

1536–40 Henry VIII closes England's monasteries.

1545–63 The Catholic Council of Trent holds numerous meetings.

1547 Henry VIII dies and Edward VI takes the English throne, establishing a Protestant kingdom.

1553 Edward VI dies; the Catholic Mary I takes the throne after the ill-fated nine-day reign of the Protestant Jane Grey.

1554 Mary I marries Philip II, heir to the Spanish throne.

February 1555 Mary I orders the burning at the stake of English subjects who refuse to accept Catholicism as their religion; in all three hundred Protestants are burned for their beliefs.

1558 Mary I dies; Elizabeth I takes the throne.

January 14, 1559 Elizabeth I makes her royal entry into the city of London on the eve of her coronation.

1559 Elizabeth establishes the Anglican Church, or the Church of England, with Parliament's approval.

1561 The Catholic Mary Stuart returns from France to take her place as the queen of a now-Protestant Scotland.

1562 English seaman John Hawkins begins a slave trade between Africa and the New World.

1562–89 The French Wars of Religion.

1564 Playwright William Shakespeare is born in Stratford-upon-Avon.

1567 The Scottish lords rise up against Mary Stuart for her scandalous behavior; she gives up the Scottish throne to her infant son and flees to England.

1568–1648 Eighty Years' War between Spain and the Netherlands.

1569 In the Northern Rising, Catholic rebels attempt to place Mary Stuart on the English throne.

1570 The Catholic pope issues a bull proclaiming that Elizabeth is not the rightful queen of England. He encourages English Catholics to rise up against her and to help Mary Stuart take the throne.

1570 The Church of England orders all major churches to obtain a copy of Foxe's *Book of Martyrs.*.

1571 Elizabeth's government foils the Ridolfi scheme, in which English Catholics backed by the Roman Catholic church and Spain attempt to rise up against Elizabeth.

1572 Nicholas Hilliard paints his first portrait miniature of Queen Elizabeth, establishing a popular English art form.

1572 St. Batholomew's Day massacre.

1575 Elizabeth grants a monopoly on printing music to royal musicians William Byrd and Thomas Tallis.

1576 Actor James Burbage erects England's first permanent structure designed specifically for staging plays, calling it simply The Theater.

1577 Explorer Francis Drake sets out on his historic round-the-world voyage.

1580 The Catholic pope calls for the murder of Elizabeth I.

1580 Philip II of Spain begins to assemble a large naval fleet, the Spanish Armada.

1584–94 A small group of top professional playwrights arises in London; they are known as the University Wits.

1585 The ill-fated Roanoke, Virginia, colony is directed and financed by Walter Raleigh under a patent by Queen Elizabeth I to colonize America.

1586 Elizabeth sends English troops to support the Dutch uprising against Spain.

1587 Playwright Christopher Marlowe writes *Tamburlaine,* the first English tragedy to effectively use blank verse.

1588 The Spanish Armada sails into the English channel with a mission to invade England. After major sea fighting between the English and Spanish, storms end the confrontation with heavy losses for the Spanish.

August 18, 1588 Elizabeth I gives her famous victory speech at Tilbury.

1588 Thomas Harriot, who was with the expedition to Roanoke, publishes *A Briefe and True Report,* the first book in English to describe the Americas.

1590 Edmund Spenser publishes the first three books of his epic poem *The Faerie Queene.*

1591 Philip Sydney's sonnet sequence *Astrophil and Stella* is published after the poet's death.

1594–97 England's crops fail due to three seasons in a row of bad weather; a famine sets in.

1594–1603 England and Ireland fight the Nine Years War.

1599 Elizabeth sends her favorite companion, Robert Devereux, to Ireland to command England's forces in the war against the Irish rebels. Devereux badly botches the mission.

1600–01 Shakespeare writes *Hamlet,* which will become the most frequently performed, read, and discussed play in the English language.

1601 England enacts a stronger version of its poor laws in an attempt to combat growing poverty.

March 24, 1603 Elizabeth I dies after ruling England for forty-five years. James VI of Scotland takes the throne as James I of England.

Words to Know

alchemy: A science of medieval times that attempted to transform base metals into gold and find a potion for eternal life.

allegory: A story or painting that represents abstract ideas or principles as characters, figures, or events.

alliteration: Repetition of the same consonant at the beginning of words or syllables.

amphitheater: A large, semi-circular outdoor theater with seats rising in tiers from a central acting area.

angel: A spiritual being ranking superior to humans, but at the lowest level of heavenly beings.

ambassador: A high-ranking official who represents his or her own country to the government of another country.

archangel: A spiritual being ranked above the angels.

archbishop: The head bishop of a province or district.

armada: The Spanish word for a fleet of ships.

astrology: The study of the position of stars and planets in the belief that they influence human affairs and events on Earth.

astronomy: The scientific study of the stars, planets, and other celestial bodies.

bishop: A clergyman with a rank higher than a priest, who has the power to ordain priests and usually presides over a diocese.

blank verse: A type of poetry with regular meter (the pattern of stressed and unstressed syllables) but no rhyme.

bull: A written communication from the pope to all Catholics worldwide.

bureaucracy: Staff of administrative officials.

capitalism: An economic system in which private individuals or companies own and invest in the country's businesses and industries with little government control.

cardinal: A top official in the Roman Catholic Church, ranking just below the pope.

cartography: Mapmaking.

chiaroscuro: In drawing or painting, a method of depicting depth and space by contrasting light and dark and creating shadows.

civic: Relating to the rights and duties of citizens.

classical: Of or relating to the art, literature, architecture, and way of life of ancient Greece or Rome, roughly between 500 BCE and 500 CE.

clergy: Authorized religious leaders, such as priests and ministers.

colony: A group of people who settle far from home but remain at least partially under the rule of their homeland.

comedy: Plays written in a light and amusing manner that present the struggles and eventual successes of everyday heroes as they overcome non-life-threatening problems.

coronation: The crowning ceremony in which a monarch officially becomes king or queen.

courtier: A person who serves or participates in the royal court or household as the king's or queen's advisor, officer, or attendant.

dignitary: A person of high rank or importance.

diocese: A large church district made up of many parishes that falls under the administration of a bishop.

doctrine: A principle (or set of principles) held by a religious or philosophical group.

Elizabethan Era: The period associated with the reign of Queen Elizabeth I (1558–1603) that is often considered to be a golden age in English history.

empirical scientist: A scientific researcher who relies on observation and experiments rather than theory.

epic: A long poem that relates the deeds of a hero and is of particular importance to a culture or nation.

episcopal: Governed by bishops.

etiquette: The conduct expected to be followed in a social or official environment.

evangelical: A member of a Protestant group that believes salvation can be attained only through faith in Christ's sacrifice and God's mercy; that the Bible, particularly the first four books of the New Testament, is the supreme authority; and that people can achieve faith only through personal experience and preaching rather than through ceremonies and rituals.

famine: The scarcity of food causing widespread hunger and starvation.

farce: Comedy that presents absurd characters and scenes in order to make the audience laugh.

feudal lord: The landowner and ruler of a district during the Middle Ages (c. 500–c. 1500) to whom the villagers owed loyalty, military service, and labor.

fresco: A painting done on wet plaster.

gentry: Landowners who did not hold titles but were from influential families.

heliocentric: Relating to the principle that the sun is the center of the solar system, with the planets rotating around it.

heresy: A religious opinion that conflicts with the church's doctrines.

heretic: Someone who expresses an opinion that opposes established church doctrines.

hierarchy: Ranking, or classification, of beings according to some standard, such as ability, importance, or social standing.

history chronicle: A play based on historic people or events.

Holy Roman Empire: A loose confederation of states and territories, including the German states and most of central Europe, that existed from 962 to 1806 and was considered the supreme political body of the Christian people.

humanism: A cultural and intellectual movement during the Renaissance, following the rediscovery of the art and literature of ancient Greece and Rome, that focused on human values, interests, and welfare.

hypothesis: An explanation of natural phenomenon that has not yet been tested; a theory.

iambic foot: A unit of poetic meter that consists of one unstressed syllable followed by one stressed syllable, as in the sound of da-DUM.

iambic pentameter: A poetic line that contains five iambic units.

iconoclasm: The deliberate destruction of religious icons (sacred images, statues, objects, and monuments) usually for religious or political reasons.

idolatry: The worship of religious icons (sacred images, statues, objects, and monuments).

knight: A man granted a rank of honor by the monarch for his personal merit or service to the country.

lady-in-waiting: A woman in the queen's household who attends the queen.

latitude: Imaginary lines that run from east to west on the globe measuring the angular distance north or south from the Earth's equator, measured in degrees.

lay person: A person who is not a member of the clergy.

longitude: Imaginary lines drawn on globes or maps that run from north to south, measuring angular distance east or west of the prime meridian, measured in degrees.

lute: A plucked string instrument similar to a guitar but shaped like a pear, with six to thirteen strings and a deep round back.

madrigal: A polyphonic love song for four to six voices without musical accompaniment.

malnutrition: Ill health caused by not eating enough food or not eating the proper balance of nutrients.

martyr: A person who chooses to be punished or put to death rather than to abandon his or her religious beliefs.

masque: A short drama, usually full of music and dance, that presents an allegory.

meter: The pattern of stressed and unstressed syllables in poetry.

Middle Ages: The period of European history between ancient times and the Renaissance (c. 500–c. 1500).

missionary: A person sent by his or her church to help people of other countries and to convert nonbelievers to the church's doctrines.

monopoly: The exclusive right to trade with a particular market or group of markets.

mortality rate: The frequency of deaths in proportion to a specific population.

mystery play: A play enacting a scene or scenes from the Bible.

nationalism: Patriotism and loyalty to a person's own country.

navigation: The science of setting the course or direction of a ship to get it from one location to another.

nobles: Elite men and women who held social titles.

P

pageant: A dramatic presentation, such as a play, that often depicts a historical, biblical, or traditional event.

papal legate: A representative of the pope within a particular nation.

parish: The community served by one local church.

patron: Someone who financially sponsors, or supports, an artist, entertainer, or explorer.

patronage system: A system in which a person with a lot of power or wealth grants favors to, financially supports, enters into contracts with, or appoints to office people who in return must promise to give their political support or access to their artistic achievements.

peasant: A class of farmers who worked in the fields owned by wealthy lords. Part of the crop was paid to the lord as rent.

peer: A noble holding the title of duke, marquis, earl, viscount, or baron.

perspective: An artistic technique used to make a two-dimensional (flat) representation appear to be three-dimensional by considering how the objects within the picture relate to one another.

pious: Highly devoted to one's religion.

polyphony: Music with many voices; or the mixing together of several melodic lines at the same time in a musical composition.

presbyterian: Governed by presbyters, or church elders..

progress: A royal procession, or trip, made by a monarch and a large number of his or her attendants.

privateers: Seafarers who own and operate their own ships independently but are authorized by their government to raid the ships of enemy nations, often capturing the entire ship with all its cargo.

Privy Council: The board of advisors that carried out the administrative function of the government in matters of economy, defense, foreign policy, and law and order, and its members served as the king's or queen's chief advisors.

prose: Ordinary speech or writing; not poetry.

Protestant: A member of one of the western Christian churches that, following reform doctrines, broke away from the Roman Catholic Church in the sixteenth century.

Protestant Reformation: Also known as the Reformation; a sixteenth-century religious movement that aimed to reform the Roman Catholic Church and resulted in the establishment of Protestant churches.

Puritans: A group of Protestants who follow strict religious standards.

rational: Based on reason rather than on spiritual belief or church authority.

Reformation: A sixteenth-century religious movement that aimed to reform the Roman Catholic Church and resulted in the establishment of Protestant churches.

regent: Someone who rules for a king or queen when the monarch is absent, too young, or unable to rule.

Renaissance: The era beginning around 1350 in Europe, in which scholars turned their attention to classical Greek and Latin learning and shifted to a more rational (based on reason rather than spiritual belief or church authority) approach to philosophy, religion, and science.

retinue: Group of attendants.

revenge tragedy: A play concerned the theme of vengeance for a past wrong—usually murder.

rhyme scheme: The pattern of rhymes in a poem.

ritual: An established ceremony performed in precise ways according to the rules of the church.

romance: A literary work about improbable events involving characters that are quite different from ordinary people.

saint: A deceased person who, due to his or her exceptionally good behavior during life, receives the official blessing of the church and is believed to be capable of interceding with God to protect people on earth.

salvation: In Christianity, deliverance from sin and punishment.

scholasticism: An effort to reconcile the teachings of the ancient classical philosophers with medieval Christian theology.

secular: Non-religious.

seminary: A school similar to a university that trains students in religion, usually to prepare them to become members of the clergy.

seraphim: The top level of angels, ranking closest to God.

shire: County.

simile: A comparison between unlike things usually using the words "like" or "as".

soliloquy: A speech in which a character, alone on stage, expresses his or her thoughts aloud.

stanza: A group of lines that form a section of a poem.

sumptuary laws: Statutes regulating how extravagantly people of the various social classes could dress.

symmetrical: Balanced, with the same-sized parts on each side.

theocracy: A state governed by religious, rather than political, principles.

Tower of London: A fortress on the Thames River in London that was used as a royal residence, treasury, and, most famously, as a prison for the upper class.

tragedy: Drama of a serious nature, usually featuring an admirable but flawed hero who undergoes a serious struggle ending in a devastating downfall.

transubstantiation: In Roman Catholic doctrine, the miraculous change that occurs when a priest blesses the Eucharist (bread and wine) and it changes into the body and blood of Christ, while maintaining the appearance of bread and wine.

vagrant: A person who wanders from town to town without a home or steady employment.

virginal: A small, legless, and rectangular keyboard instrument related to the harpsichord.

Research and Activity Ideas

Research: The Tower of London

The Tower of London played a major role in the history of Elizabethan times. Research this historical building on the Internet and/or at the library and then write a report. Describe the Tower and its uses, and be sure to briefly relate its history. At what times did Elizabeth herself stay at the Tower? What other famous Elizabethans were imprisoned or executed at the Tower of London?

Classroom Discussion: Elizabethan Catholics v. Protestants

Divide the class in half. One side will represent Catholics and the other will represent Protestants from the Elizabethan Era. Begin with a thorough discussion of the differences in beliefs and practices between the two groups. Then proceed to debate on the fairness with which Elizabeth and her Anglican Church handled these differences. What was life like for Catholics in Elizabethan England? What was life like for Puritans?

Activity: Write an Elizabethan pamphlet

There were no newspapers or magazines in Elizabethan times. Nor was there any freedom of the press. People who wanted to write about the issues of the day did so in pamphlets. But they also had to be careful not to offend the queen. Choose an Elizabethan issue, such as the queen's lack of a husband, war with Spain, the situation in Ireland, or any other topic that interests you. Make your own pamphlet presenting your opinions on the subject. Remember, you could be sent to prison or executed for what you write. How does this knowledge affect what you decide to say and how you choose to say it?

Research: Draw an Elizabethan costume

Research Elizabethan clothing, focusing on pictures of Elizabethan costumes you find in books and on the Internet. You will design a typical outfit for an Elizabethan man or woman. It can be an elaborate outfit for an upper class Elizabethan, or a more humble outfit for a farmer or other member of the working class. Using a pencil on blank paper, draw each of the different elements of an Elizabethan costume (such as ruff, kirtle, smock or shift, farthingale, hosiery, shoes, hats, jewelry, and so forth). Label each garment and identify its traits such as color, cloth type, adornments, and more.

Activity: Analyze an Elizabethan sonnet

Choose an Elizabethan sonnet from among the sonnets of William Shakespeare, Philip Sidney, Fulke Greville, or Michael Drayton. Type or write down the sonnet, leaving several spaces between each line.

First, mark the rhyming pattern of the sonnet. The last syllable of the first line is the first rhyming sound. Label it (a) at the end of the line. Among the last syllables of the remaining thirteen lines, find those that rhyme with the first line and also mark them with an (a) at the end of the line. Now find the next unmarked line and identify the sound of the last syllable of the line. Mark the end of that line with a (b). Mark all lines that rhyme with (b), and then repeat this process, using the letters (c), (d), and so on, until all lines have been labeled for their rhyming pattern.

Next, mark the sonnet's meter. Each line is in iambic pentameter, meaning it is made up of five two-syllable iambs, or units, which in turn are made up of an unstressed syllable followed by a stressed syllable (as in the sound da-DUM). With a pen or pencil, place a small line after each iamb, or two-syllable unit, and then underline the stressed syllable of each iamb (e.g. da|dum) Note the variations in the stresses.

An Elizabethan sonnet's fourteen lines are divided into four units: three quatrains (four-line parts), followed by a rhymed couplet, or two lines of rhymed verse. Mark these sections on your sonnet.

Now, read the sonnet aloud, noting how the structure influences the sound and the meaning of the sonnet.

Research: Plan the royal menu

Queen Elizabeth I is planning a dinner for important representatives from other countries and wishes to impress them. Imagine you are the royal head cook, and put together a menu for the occasion, including beverages, meats, side dishes, baked goods, and desserts.

Group Activity: Watch a movie about Queen Elizabeth and her times

Elizabeth I and her times have long fascinated filmmakers. Watch a movie about Elizabeth (see Chapter 12 for a list of films). Discuss the movie among the group, focusing on how it portrays the queen and Elizabethan times. Note the surroundings, costuming, customs, and any other physical representations of the Elizabethan Era within the film. Also compare the historical events in the film with what you know. How accurate a portrayal of Elizabethan England do you think this film provides?

Research: Read a biography for a different point of view

In the young adult section of your local school or public library, find an interesting-looking biography on Mary Stuart, Queen of Scots, or King Philip II of Spain. Read the biography, noting its perspective about Elizabeth and Elizabethan England.

Elizabethan World

Almanac

The Medieval, Catholic Roots of the Elizabethan World

The Elizabethan Era took place in England during the reign of Queen Elizabeth I, from 1558 to 1603. Often considered a golden age in English history, this period marked the nation's belated step into the Renaissance, a cultural movement that was already flourishing in other parts of Europe. The Renaissance (French for "rebirth") began around 1350 in the cities of Florence, Rome, Venice, and Milan (all in present-day Italy). During this period scholars studied classical Greek and Latin philosophy, and this new focus inspired a vibrant art movement and a shift to a rational (based on reason rather than on church authority) approach to the study of the relationship between human beings and God. The introduction of Renaissance thought to early sixteenth-century England created a new optimism (hopeful outlook) there. Many historians believe this exciting age of social and cultural transition, or change, helped England to develop into the nation it is today. But it did not happen all at once. As Elizabethan England stepped one foot forward into the Renaissance, its other foot remained firmly planted in the Middle Ages. The Middle Ages (also called medieval times) spanned from c. 500 to c. 1500. This chapter will briefly examine some of the ways people in medieval, Catholic England thought and lived just before Elizabeth came to power.

The Catholic Church of the Middle Ages

By far the most influential institution of the Middle Ages was the Catholic Church—the only Christian church in western Europe. (In fact, the word "catholic" means universal.) For many centuries the Catholic Church unified, or brought together, all Christian people under a shared set of beliefs. Most of the great medieval scholars and artists dedicated their talents wholeheartedly to the church, and most of Europe's population depended upon the church on a daily basis.

WORDS TO KNOW

bishop: A clergyman with a rank higher than a priest, who has the power to ordain priests and usually presides over a diocese.

clergy: Authorized religious leaders, such as priests and ministers.

courtier: A person who serves or participates in the royal court or household as the king's or queen's advisor, officer, or attendant.

diocese: A large church district made up of many parishes that falls under the administration of a bishop.

heresy: A religious opinion that conflicts with the church's doctrines.

heretic: Someone who expresses an opinion that opposes established church doctrines.

hierarchy: Ranking, or classification, of beings according to some standard, such as ability, importance, or social standing.

parish: The community served by one local church.

peasant: A class of farmers who worked in the fields owned by wealthy lords. Part of the crop was paid to the lord as rent.

saint: A deceased person who, due to his or her exceptionally good behavior during life, receives the official blessing of the church and is believed to be capable of interceding with God to protect people on earth.

salvation: In Christianity, deliverance from sin and punishment.

transubstantiation: In Roman Catholic doctrine, the miraculous change that occurs when a priest blesses the Eucharist (bread and wine) and it changes into the body and blood of Christ, while maintaining the appearance of bread and wine.

Throughout most of the Middle Ages the Catholic Church was based in Rome. It was led by the pope, the bishop of Rome, who was considered God's representative on earth. The pope appointed the cardinals and bishops, or religious leaders, who went out to serve the various states and kingdoms of Europe under the pope's leadership.

While religious unity was a goal of the medieval church, religious tolerance was almost nonexistent. Non-Christians in western Europe fared poorly. All Jews were expelled (forced to leave) from England in 1290, and from France in 1306 and again in 1394. Those two countries—along with Germany, eastern Europe, and northern Italy— were exclusively Christian. That is, everyone who lived there was required to be a faithful member of the Catholic Church. In Spain there was growing tension between the Catholics and the Muslim Moors who ruled Granada, a province in what would soon become southern Spain. The hostilities increased until 1492, when Spain conquered Granada and united as a Catholic state, driving out all Jews and Muslims.

The order of the universe

Medieval Europeans thought of the universe as a carefully ordered place. They used a simple model called the Great Chain of Being to express this sense of order. The Great Chain can be envisioned as a huge ladder mounting up to the heavens. At the very top is God, who created all things. Below God, in descending order, are the various levels of angels, the stars, the Sun, the Moon, the planets, humans (each at a specific social level), animals (with apes at the top), plants, and finally rocks and soil. Each element in the universe took a specific place within the hierarchy, or ranking system, according to its unchanging standing in the universe. Each element also fulfilled a particular function in the world.

In the Catholic belief system, the universe had been maintained in perfect order until Adam and Eve committed the original sin by disobeying God and eating from the tree of knowledge. For their sin, God threw them out of Eden, or the earthly paradise, and doomed all their descendants to a world of change, death, and corruption. The only hope for human beings to find salvation (deliverance from the effects of sin) was to repent, or recognize their sins and try to find forgiveness. No one could be saved unless they understood and accepted the sacrifice of Jesus Christ, who died on the cross for the salvation of humankind. Catholics regularly celebrated the miracle of Christ's sacrifice. At the Catholic Mass a process called transubstantiation took place. In the transubstantiation ceremony a priest blessed bread and wine, miraculously turning it into the actual body and blood of Christ, though it continued to look like bread and wine. This ceremony was often called the Elevation of the Host, referring to the priest's raising of the wine and bread immediately after blessing it so the miracle could be seen and revered by the members of the church.

Medieval Christians believed they could only find salvation by following the guidance, laws, and teachings of the church, for according to Catholic beliefs, the church and its clergy had been proclaimed by Christ to be the only intermediary (go-between) between God and human beings. Most medieval people could not read, so they could not study the Bible for themselves. They relied on the church to explain the will of God to them. The church also instructed its members to live moderately, without seeking excessive wealth or fame, and to honorably serve their religion and their ruler. In church the faithful were taught not only the key to salvation, but also how to live as a community and accept the life into which they were born.

Medieval art often depicted the skeletal figure of Death claiming his victims. PRIVATE COLLECTION/BRIDGEMAN ART LIBRARY. REPRODUCED BY PERMISSION.

Medieval Europeans were fascinated with death in ways most modern people would find strange or even disgusting. Their art frequently represented the decomposed bodies of the dead in hideously graphic detail. Great artists painted picture after picture of the skeletal figure of Death claiming his victims. In Paris an elaborate park was created in the Cemetery of the Innocents, the burial place of hundreds of thousands of poor people. In the thirteenth century people enjoyed leisurely afternoon walks through the cemetery park, viewing the open shelves full of disintegrating human bones. The fascination with death seems to have arisen from the medieval view of life as a difficult passage that had to be endured on one's way to the afterlife. Medieval Christians hoped to be prepared for death when it came; they believed that people who died without having repented their sins and confessed them to a member of the clergy were doomed to suffer in the fires of hell forever.

Medieval churches in England

In early medieval England local churches were built and funded by noblemen, or lords who ruled over large districts. The lord appointed the parish priest, usually someone of the commoner class (something like the middle class of today), who then lived and worked at the parish church. A parish is the community served by one local church. The parish church was more than a religious institution; it was the center of village life. The parish churches took on the duty of caring for the sick and the poor. They frequently offered travelers a place to stay, and they provided whatever schooling was available in a village. They also served as centers for celebrations and ceremony.

Cathedrals were large churches that served as the seats of the bishops, the religious directors of the dioceses. A diocese is a large church district that encompasses many parishes. Cathedrals were usually magnificent buildings that brought prestige and business to the towns in which they were built. They served as places of worship and religious celebration, but they were also cultural centers that housed religious courts, marketplaces, and schools. Two famous English medieval cathedrals were at York and Canterbury.

Monasteries were communities set apart from the daily life of towns and villages in which monks, men who had pledged their lives to prayer, lived in a community together, practicing a simple and pious life and following strict rules. Women who wished to pursue a life of prayer were called nuns and lived in convents. Most English monasteries and convents were initially built in isolated (far from other communities) areas. The monasteries owned their own lands and functioned as lords, with peasants working the land for them. (Peasants were farmers who worked in the fields owned by wealthy lords. Part of the crop was paid to the lord as rent.) Monks and nuns in England taught religion but also participated in worldly enterprises, including commerce and entertainment.

Medieval cathedrals like Exeter Cathedral (shown here) were places of worship as well as cultural centers. © MICHAEL NICHOLSON/CORBIS.

The Western Schism and England's growing distrust

In 1378 a power struggle arose between two different popes who both claimed to lead the Catholic Church. One pope set up headquarters in Avignon, in present-day France, and another remained in Rome. The European states split their loyalty between the two. This split, called the Western Schism, lasted nearly forty years, until 1417. Many Europeans felt doomed during this time, believing that no one could find salvation as long as the Catholic Church was divided.

English people had traditionally been somewhat intolerant of foreigners; consequently, many of them had difficulty accepting the foreign pope as their spiritual leader. The Western Schism heightened these feelings of distrust. When it ended in 1417 many English people were unwilling to accept the pope as the supreme leader of the Catholic religion in their land. Some of the more devout English Catholics also were growing suspicious of other new trends in the Roman Catholic Church.

Over the years the church had developed many rituals through which its faithful could seek God's favor. Rituals are established ceremonies performed in precise ways according to the rules of the church. For example, someone hoping for a good harvest might purchase candles to burn for a particular saint. (A saint is a deceased person who has received the official blessing of the church and is believed to be capable of interceding with God to protect people on earth.) Someone repenting a small sin might repeat certain prayers over and over. Those who had the means might collect holy relics, such as the bones or belongings of a saint. During the Middle Ages the Virgin Mary became the object of many people's prayers for protection and comfort; many prayed directly to her image. To some scholarly Catholics of the time, these practices seemed more like superstition than religion. Superstition is the belief that there is a kind of magical power within certain practices or objects and that the future, or the outcome of certain events, can be influenced by certain behaviors.

The Catholic Church offered several ways for its wealthier members to use their money to improve their lives after they died. According to the Church all people (except saints) who were not destined for hell upon their deaths went to a middle place called purgatory. In purgatory the deceased person suffered punishment similar to the torments of hell as a means of purifying his or her soul in preparation for heaven. Unlike hell, however, the suffering in purgatory was finite (would come to an end). The length of time one spent there varied depending on the seriousness of one's sins. But the prayers of the living could shorten the time a dead person spent suffering in purgatory. For example, when someone died, a priest led a Mass to pray for the release of the person's soul from purgatory. Family members were expected to continue these prayers well after the death. To ensure their prompt release from purgatory, people began to leave large sums of money to the churches to pay for prayers to be said for their souls after their deaths. Wealthy people invested in chantries, which were private chapels they endowed with enough funds to pay for priests or monks to say daily masses for them for many decades after their death.

In the later Middle Ages people who had sinned could also use their money to purchase papal indulgences. These were fines imposed by the church on people who had sinned and repented, and the church viewed

The Lollards

In 1366 John Wycliffe (c. 1320–1384), a philosopher, theologian (one who studies religion and the nature of religious truth), and priest who taught at the University of Oxford, called for England to separate from the current pope and take control of its own Catholic Church. Wycliffe did not believe the huge and wealthy institutions in Rome or Avignon comprised the Catholic Church. He defined the church simply as the combined souls of all faithful Christians. According to Wycliffe the pope was failing to serve the church adequately. The pope, in turn, accused Wycliffe of heresy, an opinion that conflicts with the church's doctrines. The pope's anger did not concern the English government, which until that time had no real experience with heresy. Despite the pope's accusation Wycliffe was allowed to continue teaching at Oxford.

In 1380 Wycliffe began to criticize the Catholic doctrine of transubstantiation. Wycliffe argued that what took place in the ceremony—changing bread and wine to the flesh and blood of Christ—represented a miracle but it was not in itself a miracle. He contended that God alone could perform that miracle, not human priests. Later he argued against the Catholic practice of confessing one's sins to a priest, asserting that only God had the power to absolve (pardon) people of sin. In effect Wycliffe contended that priests had no more authority than other believers.

Wycliffe played a large role in the first translation of the Bible from Latin to English in the 1380s. The Catholic Church held that it was the function of the church to interpret and teach the Bible to its followers, and it opposed translations. Wycliffe believed that ordinary English people should be able to study the Bible individually in order to appreciate the word of God. To spread readings of the Bible throughout the populace, Wycliffe sent out his

John Wycliffe. KEAN COLLECTION/GETTY IMAGES.

followers, who were called Lollards, as traveling preachers. Wycliffe hoped that the Lollards, who lived in poverty and had no official connection to the church, would eventually replace the existing church hierarchy.

Long after Wycliffe's death, the Lollards continued to gather secretly to study the translated Bible. As there were only a few dozen English-language Bibles, many Lollards memorized large portions of it and thus brought it to others. The existing English-language Bibles were carefully passed from generation to generation. Many Lollards became more radical, or ready to make drastic changes, in their religion than their founder, Wycliffe, had been. They caused enough concern in England that Parliament passed an act to burn heretics, or people who opposed the established Roman Catholic doctrines, at the stake. In fact, two Lollards were burned at the stake for their beliefs, but the movement was small and did not become a major issue in England. The Roman Catholic establishment continued to be troubled by the existence of the Lollards, though, and in 1428, the pope ordered Wycliffe's bones to be dug up, smashed, and scattered as punishment for his rejection of the church's authority.

them as a way to atone, or pay, for one's sins. Critics noted that they also had the effect of filling the church treasury.

By the 1400s the Catholic Church in England had, indeed, become very wealthy. Many bishops, priests, and monks who in prior times might have spent their time in prayer were more often spending their time on the tremendous business operations of the church. While some monasteries quietly performed their devoted religious work, others became corrupt. A few were shamefully immoral and others simply neglected their purpose. Most English people remained perfectly content to worship in their parish churches, but some found it increasingly difficult to respect the teachings of piety and moderation from a clergy involved in worldly pursuits.

The Renaissance begins

In Europe a new movement called the Renaissance developed during the fourteenth century, initially stemming from the works of the Italian poet and scholar Francesco Petrarch (1304–1374). His enthusiasm for classic Latin writings eventually spread from Italy to all of western Europe. The study of classical texts, philosophy, and religion came to be known as humanism. The classical texts introduced scholars to a new way of viewing the world. Medieval Europeans had believed that the meaning of life on Earth lay primarily in its relation to an afterlife. They valued the arts only if they had a religious purpose. The new Renaissance humanists challenged the blind acceptance of authority that had been the standard of the past. Renaissance humanists encouraged the individual to search for truth through human reason. They valued earthly life and glorified human nature.

One of the most important advances of the Renaissance was the invention of the printing press by Johannes Gutenberg (c. 1398–1468) in the 1450s. The first press, a mechanism in which small metal pieces engraved with single characters could be arranged to form words and

Johannes Gutenberg (center) reviews a newly printed manuscript. Gutenberg's invention of the printing press was one of the first major advances of the Renaissance.
© BETTMANN/CORBIS.

sentences, was used in Germany to print the Latin translation of the Bible. Soon presses appeared all over Europe, with enormous impact. Literacy (the ability to read) grew and knowledge spread as the printed word became readily available to many people for the first time. To some the large-scale production of the Gutenberg Bible brought about a welcome change in religion, for it meant that every person could discover Christian salvation through his or her own understanding of the Bible individually—without the help of the church.

By the late fifteenth century, many humanists had begun to study the Bible, initiating a reform movement. The reformers were generally well-read, pious people who wished only to improve the Catholic Church—not to start their own church. One leading early-sixteenth-century reformer was the Dutch-born humanist Desiderius Erasmus (1466–1536). Erasmus applied his knowledge of classical civilization to pre-medieval Christianity. He felt that medieval Christian scholars had corrupted the faith, making doctrines too complicated and too difficult to understand. Erasmus produced his own translation of the New Testament and wrote *In Praise of Folly* (1509), a satire of the clergy, scholars, and philosophers of his day. A satire is a literary work in which human folly is ridiculed through irony or humor. English statesman Sir Thomas More (1478–1535) shared Erasmus's frustration and also wrote satires hoping to reform the practices of the church and the clergy.

For More Information

BOOKS

Brigden, Susan. *New Worlds, Lost Worlds: The Rule of the Tudors, 1485–1603.* New York: Penguin Books, 2000.

Schama, Simon. *A History of Britain: At the Edge of the World? 3500 BC –1603 AD.* New York: Hyperion, 2000.

Smith, Lacey Baldwin. *The Elizabethan Epic.* London: Panther, 1966.

Tillyard, E. M. W. *The Elizabethan World Picture.* New York: Vintage Books, 1942.

WEB SITES

"The Middle Ages." *E-Museum at Minnesota State University, Mankato.* http://www.mnsu.edu/emuseum/history/middleages/ (accessed on July 11, 2006).

Muhlberger, Steven. *The ORB: On-line Reference Book for Medieval Studies.* http://www.the-orb.net/textbooks/muhlberger/muhlindex.html (accessed on July 11, 2006).

2

The Reformation in England

The Protestant Reformation, a religious movement that aimed to reform the Roman Catholic Church and resulted in the establishment of Protestant churches, began in the early sixteenth century when German monk Martin Luther (1483–1546) publicized his objections to the practices of the Catholic Church. Luther believed that faith in Christ, not the intervention of the church, was the route to salvation (deliverance from the results of sin). Luther argued that the Bible—not the Catholic Church—was the sole spiritual authority. He was particularly disgusted by the sale of papal indulgences, or free passes issued by the pope to wealthy people, allowing them to sin and then pay to be forgiven. Luther believed only God could forgive sins.

On October 31, 1517, Luther is said to have nailed to the church door in Wittenberg (a city in present-day Germany) a list of ninety-five theses, or statements, attacking the use of papal indulgences and inviting debate on the subject. He also began to write and distribute pamphlets about his views. When people from all walks of life began to support Luther and his ideas, the officials of the Catholic Church demanded that he repudiate, or withdraw, his views. When he refused, the church declared him an outlaw and sentenced him to death. Luther went into hiding, but he emerged in 1522 to find that almost half the people of the German states had adopted his views and were calling themselves Lutherans.

England's introduction to Protestantism

While the Protestant Reformation movement spread swiftly through parts of Europe in the 1520s, at first it appealed to very few residents of the geographically isolated island of England. The country had a long-standing but small group of reformers called evangelicals, who believed that salvation could be attained only through faith in Christ's sacrifice

WORDS TO KNOW

archbishop: The head bishop of a province or district.

bishop: A clergyman with a rank higher than a priest, who has the power to ordain priests and usually presides over a diocese.

cardinal: A top official in the Roman Catholic Church, ranking just below the pope.

clergy: Authorized religious leaders, such as priests and ministers.

courtier: A person who serves or participates in the royal court or household as the king's or queen's advisor, officer, or attendant.

doctrine: A principle (or set of principles) held by a religious or philosophical group.

evangelical: A member of a Protestant group that believes salvation can be attained only through faith in Christ's sacrifice and God's mercy; that the Bible, particularly the first four books of the New Testament, is the supreme authority; and that people can achieve faith only through personal experience and preaching rather than through ceremonies and rituals.

heresy: A religious opinion that conflicts with the church's doctrines.

Holy Roman Empire: A loose confederation of states and territories, including the German states and most of central Europe, that existed from 962 to 1806 and was considered the supreme political body of the Christian people.

lady-in-waiting: A woman in the queen's household who attends the queen.

papal legate: A representative of the pope within a particular nation.

Protestant: A member of one of the western Christian churches that, following reform doctrines, broke away from the Roman Catholic Church in the sixteenth century.

Reformation: A sixteenth-century religious movement that aimed to reform the Roman Catholic Church and resulted in the establishment of Protestant churches.

regent: Someone who rules for a king or queen when the monarch is absent, too young, or unable to rule.

ritual: An established ceremony performed in precise ways according to the rules of the church.

salvation: In Christianity, deliverance from sin and punishment.

Tower of London: A fortress on the Thames River in London that was used as a royal residence, treasury, and, most famously, as a prison for the upper class.

transubstantiation: In Roman Catholic doctrine, the miraculous change that occurs when a priest blesses the Eucharist (bread and wine) and it changes into the body and blood of Christ, while maintaining the appearance of bread and wine.

and God's mercy; that the Bible was the supreme authority; and that people could achieve faith only through personal experience and preaching rather than through ceremonies and rituals. Most English people, however, were not interested in the evangelical movement. England's introduction to the Reformation came with a jolt in the 1530s, when the country abruptly broke with the Catholic Church as a result of King Henry VIII's (1491–1547; reigned 1509–47) desire for a divorce. Henry's actions, which had nothing to do with the ideas of Martin Luther, prompted a chain of events that would lead to religious upheaval during his kingship and the reigns of his three children, Edward VI (1537–1553; reigned 1547–53), Mary I (1516–1558; reigned 1553–58), and Elizabeth I (1533–1603; reigned 1558–1603).

Henry VIII, Defender of the Faith

Henry VIII was the second son of Henry VII (1457–1509; reigned 1485–1509) and Elizabeth of York (1466–1503). His older brother, Arthur, was expected to succeed his father as king. While Henry was still a young boy, his parents arranged for Arthur to marry Catherine of Aragon (1485–1536), the daughter of the king and queen of Spain. This marriage, undertaken for the purpose of maintaining a strong alliance between Spain and England, took place in 1501, but Arthur died shortly after the wedding. The king, still pursuing the alliance, decided to marry his younger son, Henry, to Catherine. Because of a Biblical prohibition against marrying one's brother's wife, Henry was forced to obtain a dispensation (permission) from the pope for the marriage. In the end, the marriage did not take place until after Henry VII's death. The seventeen-year-old Henry married Catherine as he took the English throne in 1509.

The new king was intelligent, forceful, and highly charismatic (having a strong magnetic charm), but he was also selfish, egotistical, and often cruel. Henry VIII's primary goal was to make England a major power comparable to any in Europe. He spent a great deal of time, money, and human lives waging wars with France and Scotland. When not concerned with matters of war, he preferred to spend his time hunting, playing music, and carousing with his courtiers (people who serve or participate in the royal court or household as the king's advisors, officers, or attendants). He left many of the duties of state to his Lord Chancellor (the king's highest officer), Thomas Wolsey (c. 1475–1530). Wolsey attained great power, becoming a Catholic cardinal (a top official in the Roman Catholic Church, ranking just below the pope) and a papal legate, or a representative of the pope within a particular nation. Soon he was the most powerful man in the country next to the king, and he became extremely rich, building some of England's largest palaces and

Catholic cardinal Thomas Wolsey became one of the most powerful men in England during the early part of the reign of King Henry VIII.
HULTON ARCHIVE/GETTY IMAGES.

living in luxury. Many nobles resented his wealth and power, viewing it as an example of the corruption of the Catholic Church.

When Martin Luther's teachings began to reach English shores in the 1520s, Henry labeled them heresy (religious opinion that conflicts with the church's doctrines, or principles). In 1521, with the help of one of his favored councilors, the renowned writer and statesman Thomas More (1478–1535), Henry wrote and published *Defense of the Seven Sacraments,* an argument against Luther's ideas. For this work the Catholic pope honored him with the title "Defender of the Faith."

At that time, one of the leading English evangelical reformers, William Tyndale (1494–1536), decided to produce a new English translation of the Bible and distribute it to the English people. The Catholic Church banned all translations in the belief that it was the church's role to instruct its members about the teachings of the Bible. Tyndale, fearing prosecution in England, carried out his mission of translation and printing in the German city of Worms. In 1526 he secretly shipped to London three thousand copies of an English translation of the New Testament. As these books surfaced, Henry VIII and Wolsey staged a massive book-burning, destroying as many copies of the translated Bible as they could find. They warned the reformers that in the future their bodies would be burned at the stake, along with any heretical books found in their presence.

King Henry's "great matter"

In the meantime, though, Henry was trying to father a male heir to take the throne upon his death. With Catherine, however, he had only one surviving child, Mary, and he wanted a boy to succeed him. By the late 1520s, with Catherine past her childbearing years, Henry was desperate to resolve what became known as "the king's great matter." He began to believe he had been cursed with a lack of sons as punishment for going against the teachings of the Bible and marrying his brother's wife. His anxiety to divorce Catherine intensified around 1527, when he fell in love with Anne Boleyn (c. 1504–1536), a lady-in-waiting to his wife. (A lady-in-waiting is a woman in the queen's household who attends the queen.) Anne refused to become Henry's mistress, and the lovesick king decided to marry her and make her queen of England.

Although Catholic doctrine did not allow for divorce, termination of marriages among kings was not unusual. Wolsey asked the pope to annul Henry's marriage to Catherine, arguing that the marriage was illegitimate because Catherine had been Arthur's widow. But Catherine protested, saying she and Arthur had never consummated their marriage (had sexual relations). Catherine's nephew, Charles V (1500–1558), the Holy Roman Emperor, had great influence over the pope and was able to stop him from terminating his aunt's marriage. (The title of Holy Roman Emperor is granted by the pope to the person who led, at least in name, the states and territories within the Holy Roman Empire, a loose confederation of states and territories including the German states and most of central Europe.) By 1529 it was clear that the pope would not agree to

Henry VIII divorced his wife to marry Anne Boleyn. The Catholic Church would not grant the divorce, so Henry broke with the church and declared himself head of the church in England. © HISTORICAL PICTURE ARCHIVE/CORBIS.

Henry's demands. The angry king fired Wolsey from his position as lord chancellor.

Cromwell and Cranmer

Two new advisors on Henry's council, Thomas Cranmer (1489–1556) and Thomas Cromwell (1489–1540), quickly gained power after Wolsey's dismissal. Both were Protestants, and many historians consider them the architects of the English Reformation. Cromwell and Cranmer both took advantage of the king's desire for a divorce to get into his good graces. Each worked in his own way—Cranmer through the church and Cromwell through the government. They began by convincing the king that England was an empire (a large political body made up of several territories or groups of people under a single, all-powerful leader). As emperor, they explained, Henry was the supreme leader of both state and church and therefore not subject to the authority of the pope or the Catholic Church in Rome.

Cromwell brought the matter of the Henry's role in the church before Parliament, the legislative body in England. Many members of Parliament had been so outraged at the power Wolsey had achieved through his connections with Rome that they were glad to work toward a break with the pope. Under Cromwell and Cranmer's influence, the Reformation Parliament, which sat for seven years beginning in 1529, created a series of acts that cut the ties between England and the Catholic Church in Rome. Under Cromwell's fierce pressure, in 1531 the English clergy accepted Henry as the head of the church in England.

In 1532 Cranmer was appointed Archbishop of Canterbury, the chief religious leader in England. The king had arranged the appointment because he expected Cranmer, as head of the church, to annul his marriage to Catherine. Indeed, things had become a little more urgent for the king—Anne Boleyn was pregnant. Henry was certain the child was a son and wanted him to be legitimate; that is, born to married parents. Though not yet divorced, he had married Anne in secret and brought her into the royal court as if she were queen. As soon as he became Archbishop of Canterbury, Cranmer carried out Henry's wishes. He declared Henry's marriage to Catherine of Aragon invalid and then publicly affirmed that Henry's marriage to Anne Boleyn had been lawful and crowned Anne as queen of England. Henry had gotten his way. His excommunication (being deprived of church membership) from the Catholic Church followed Anne's coronation, or crowning as queen.

When Anne's child, the future Queen Elizabeth I, was born in September 1533, Henry was deeply disappointed to learn that she was a girl, but the course for England had already been set. In March 1534 Parliament passed the Act of Succession, which made the children of Henry and Anne the future heirs to the English throne, and effectively proclaimed his daughter, Mary, illegitimate. The act required the English people to pledge their loyalty to the succession of the new queen's children and to Henry's role as the supreme head of the English church. That same year Parliament passed the Act of Treason, making it a crime punishable by death to dispute the king's religious rulings. Anyone who refused to go along with the succession act or the supremacy act was

Calvinism

French scholar John Calvin (1509–1564) led the second generation of Protestant reformers in the 1530s and became the most influential Protestant leader of his time. Calvin had read and admired the works of Martin Luther, and in most respects their theology was the same. Like Luther and many earlier theologians, Calvin believed that all human beings were sinful from birth and he denied that humans have free will, arguing that God had determined every soul's fate at the beginning of time. Calvin believed that God chose only a special few, whom he called "the elect," for salvation. But while earlier theologians held that people who did not find salvation were responsible for their own fate because of their sins, Calvin argued there was nothing a human could do, whether good or evil, to influence God's will. God had already determined who would be saved and who would be damned. Aware of the gloomy aspect of this doctrine—the belief that it makes no difference what one does in life, since one's fate has already been determined—Calvin proclaimed that those who lived a good Christian life should assume they were among the elect.

Calvin went further than Luther in criticizing the Catholic Church, particularly in regard to the Catholic doctrine of transubstantiation, the miraculous change that occurs in a Catholic mass when a priest blesses the Eucharist elements, bread and wine, and they change to become the body and blood of Christ, while maintaining the appearance of bread and wine. While Luther held that no priest could achieve such a miracle, he believed that Christ was physically present in the Eucharist during the Mass. Calvin disagreed, calling the presence of Christ at the mass merely spiritual, a way for people to remember and celebrate the miracle. There were other differences between Lutherans and Calvinists as well.

Protestant reformer John Calvin. COURTESY OF THE LIBRARY OF CONGRESS.

While Lutherans retained the ceremonial worship of the Catholic Church, following precise steps and using traditional objects of worship, Calvin introduced a simple, austere service in which the sermon, not the ceremony or objects, was central. Lutheranism became the main form of Protestantism in Germany and Scandinavia, while Calvinism became the Protestant doctrine in Switzerland, France, the Netherlands, and Scotland.

For a time Calvin led the Protestant movement from the city of Geneva (in present-day Switzerland). Calvin attempted to turn Geneva into a city of model Christians. He introduced and rigidly enforced strict laws on daily conduct based on the teachings of the church. Geneva became a center of the Reformation. A school Calvin founded at Geneva in 1559 became the training ground of hundreds of Protestant pastors from all nations. The city was a haven for persecuted Protestants from all over Europe. Calvin's followers carried his teachings to eager reformers throughout Europe, especially in France, where Calvinists were called Huguenots, and in England, where they inspired the Puritan movement.

charged with treason. Among those who refused was Henry's once-favored councilor, Thomas More (1478–1535), who was executed for his beliefs in 1535.

Anne Boleyn reigned as Henry's queen for two-and-a-half years, but by 1536, when Anne had not produced a son, Henry was convinced his marriage had been a mistake. The ever-faithful Cromwell began arresting most of the men who had access to the queen. Under torture, a musician in her household was forced to confess to sexual relations with the queen. Although few believed the charges, Anne Boleyn was arrested for treason (adultery in connection with a king was considered treason). Henry then had Cranmer declare that his marriage with Anne had been illegitimate since he had been married to Catherine when it took place. Two days later Anne Boleyn was beheaded. Within two weeks of Anne's death, Henry married Jane Seymour (c. 1509–1537), a lady-in-waiting to Anne. She would, at last, produce the desired male heir, Edward, though she died in the process.

Dissolution of the monasteries

Though the king was by no means a Protestant, he supported some evangelical reforms when it suited him. Many of England's monasteries (houses for monks or nuns who live under religious vows) had become extremely wealthy, owning vast lands, fine buildings, and art and treasures worth a fortune. In 1536 Henry and Cromwell began to close the smaller monasteries. It was a popular measure among the Protestants and others who believed the monasteries were corrupt. For Henry this reform effort had the obvious benefit of filling up his royal treasury with the monasteries' fortunes. (The Crown received all the goods within the religious houses, while the local nobles received the land and buildings.) About 160 of the smaller monasteries were shut down that year.

Not everyone was pleased with the king's actions against the Catholic Church, however. In the strongly Catholic population in northern

England, the closing of the monasteries caused several uprisings. In 1536 a large rebellion known as the Pilgrimage of Grace took shape in Yorkshire. About forty thousand rebels participated. By deceiving the rebels into thinking the king would agree to their concerns, the king's army eventually defeated the angry mob. Still, Henry and Cromwell, not satisfied with closing the small monasteries, went after the rest. By 1540 about 250 large monasteries had been closed. The dissolution of the monasteries greatly enriched the English Crown and garnered Henry enormous support from the nobles who had received the monasteries' estates.

Henry's last years

Henry was to marry three more times after the death of Jane Seymour. Cromwell arranged a marriage between Henry and the German princess Anne of Cleves (c. 1515–1557), a Protestant. The marriage did not please Henry. He had it annulled and, blaming Cromwell for the ordeal, fired him. Cromwell was executed on some questionable charges a year later. In 1540 Henry married the teenaged Catherine Howard (c. 1525–1542), Anne Boleyn's cousin, who later was accused of adultery and executed for treason. Henry's sixth and last marriage was to Katherine Parr (c. 1512–1548), who nursed the sick and aging king through his last years. Parr served as a warm and loving stepmother to his two younger children, Elizabeth and Edward. She was intrigued with evangelical reform and held daily religious study classes at court. Both of her stepchildren attended this instruction eagerly and were therefore in regular contact with some of the prominent Protestant reformers of the time.

After dismissing Cromwell, Henry controlled the church in England more directly, fully utilizing his power as the head of the church to decide what was doctrine and what was heresy. His Act of Six Articles (1539) reinstated certain Catholic traditions that had been discontinued under Protestant reform, affirming the Catholic doctrine of transubstantiation, as well as the practice of confessing one's sins to a priest. Two Protestant influences remained: the availability of the English translation of the Bible and having the king, not the pope, as the head of the church. Henry did not allow people to pick and choose which church doctrines to follow. Under the act heresy was punishable by death by burning. Catholics who could not accept Henry as the head of the church were executed, along with Protestants who denied the doctrine of transubstantiation. It was a confusing and frightening time for people on both sides of the issue. Catholics feared that the fate of their souls might be doomed for all eternity because of the break with Rome. Some Protestants chose to be burned at the stake rather than agree to Catholic doctrines. Most people learned to be silent about their true beliefs, hoping for better days to come.

Protestant rule: 1547–1553

When Henry died in 1547, his ten-year-old son succeeded to the throne as Edward VI. Edward's uncle, Edward Seymour, Earl of Hertford (c. 1506–1552; later Duke of Somerset), received authority to act as regent (someone who rules for a king or queen when the monarch is absent, too young, or unable to rule). Seymour was a Protestant, and the Protestant Thomas Cranmer remained Archbishop of Canterbury. The young Edward was thoroughly Protestant himself, and so a way was open for the Reformation to establish itself in England.

One of the first acts of Edward's government was to repeal his father's hated heresy statutes. There were no burnings at the stake on matters of religion during his reign. In 1548 Somerset instituted the first Act of Uniformity, prescribing a new service for all English churches as described in the *Book of Common Prayer,* written by Cranmer. The book changed the transubstantiation rite into a celebration of the sacrifice of Christ that did not actually repeat the miracle of his Resurrection (rising from death), as it had in Catholic practice. The new mass was to be called Holy Communion, and it was delivered in English rather than Latin. Many of the Catholic decorations in churches, such as stained glass windows and statues of the Virgin Mary, were removed. The new look in English churches was starkly plain, reflecting the simple piety of Protestant worship.

Somerset soon fell from power and was replaced by John Dudley, Earl of Warwick (1502–1553; later Duke of Northumberland), as Edward's chief councilor. Northumberland was eager to push Protestant reforms. Under his direction all Catholic service books were banned. England's Catholic bishops were dismissed from the church and replaced by Protestant bishops, such as Hugh Latimer, Bishop of Worcester (1485–1555), and Nicholas Ridley, Bishop of Rochester (1500–1555), who sought extensive evangelical reforms. Cranmer, though, continued to move slowly to educate the English public about the reformed church, using a mix of traditional Catholic and contemporary Protestant doctrine. He feared that sudden changes might confuse or even turn some away from their religion. Both Catholics and Protestants fiercely resisted his methods, but the young king Edward supported him. The archbishop produced a second *Prayer Book* (1552), a more outwardly Protestant book of church services that required every English citizen to attend the reformed service. He also wrote the *Forty-Two Articles*, a set of Reformation church doctrines. Cranmer's efforts would later become the basis for Elizabeth I's religious settlement and the Anglican Church. (For more information on the establishment of the Anglican Church, see Chapter 3.)

The nine-day reign of Jane Grey

In early 1553 Edward's health was deteriorating rapidly. Historians suggest that he may have been suffering from tuberculosis, a disease of the lungs. Northumberland, knowing that Edward was near death, was concerned that if Mary, a devout Catholic, succeeded him, she would be sure to undo all his Protestant reforms. Northumberland devised a plan. Henry's will had stated that if all three of his children died without heirs, the throne would go to his sister's descendants, the Greys. Northumberland quickly arranged a marriage between one of these descendants, the seventeen-year-old Jane Grey (1537–1554), and his own son. He convinced the dying Edward to create a will leaving the rule of England to Jane Grey. Although it would have taken an act of Parliament to make Edward's will effective, Northumberland managed to persuade the other royal councilors to back his plan to put his new daughter-in-law on the throne.

When Edward died at the age of fifteen, Northumberland brought a reluctant Jane Grey to the royal court as queen. The people of London were grimly silent as she was escorted past them. Mary Tudor, the daughter of Catherine of Aragon, had their overwhelming support. Catholics and Protestants alike believed Mary was queen by divine (God-given) right, and considered it dangerous to replace a legitimate monarch. When Mary rode into London several days later, the city welcomed her triumphantly. Northumberland was abandoned by his army and the royal council, and Jane Grey, queen of England for just nine days, was arrested and later beheaded by order of the new queen.

Bloody Mary

Upon taking the throne the thirty-seven-year-old Mary immediately sought a husband so that she could provide an heir for England. Though her council urged her to marry an Englishman, she consulted

Mary Tudor became queen in 1553. COURTESY OF THE LIBRARY OF CONGRESS.

Charles V, the Holy Roman Emperor, for a suitable match. Charles urged her to marry his son, Prince Philip (1527–1598), heir to the Spanish throne. Mary joyfully agreed.

The English public was outraged with Mary's choice of husband. No foreigner had served as king for centuries. Rumors spread that Philip planned to make England a province of Spain once he married the queen. Plans for uprisings were widespread. In Kent, three thousand men led by Thomas Wyatt (1521–1554) headed for London, planning to kill Mary and place the princess Elizabeth on the throne. But Mary had loyal followers in London and the rebels were stopped. Wyatt and many others were gruesomely executed, their body parts hung from the walls of London to warn others against revolt. Though Mary had begun her

Protestant leaders like Thomas Cranmer were burned at the stake after refusing to convert to Catholicism under the rule of Mary I. HULTON ARCHIVE/ GETTY IMAGES.

reign with no ill will toward her Protestant subjects, after the uprising she began to believe that all reformers sought to overthrow her; consequently, all who professed Protestantism were, in her eyes, traitors to their country.

Mary and Philip were married in 1554. Mary restored the traditional Catholic Mass, requiring all English citizens to attend. The shift was awkward. English youth had never known Catholicism, and many Protestants were deeply pious and unwilling to change. Mary and her religious leaders believed that the only way to bring unity to England was to force the Protestants to recant, or change their religion. The Catholic bishops spent hours trying to force Protestants to recant through coaxing, threats, and finally torture. Those who refused to recant were condemned to die the painful death of heretics—burning at the stake. Burnings began in February 1555 in Smithfield, near London, and continued for three years. Prominent Protestants such as Thomas Cranmer, Hugh Latimer, and Nicholas Ridley, as well as hundreds of humble English men and women, suffered a heretic's death. In all, about three hundred people were burned to death during Mary's short reign. More than eight hundred Protestants left England for refuge in Protestant areas of Europe.

In 1558 Mary died of cancer. The weary people of England looked to the succession of the princess Elizabeth with a mixture of fear and hope for their spiritual future.

The Princess Elizabeth

The childhood of Henry's daughter, Elizabeth, had been full of anguish and drama. Her birth had become the reason for a break with the Roman Catholic Church, and her mother had been executed at her father's orders before the young princess was three years old. But it was not all bad. Elizabeth was educated along with her brother, Edward, by some of the top scholars from Cambridge University. Her tutors had participated in the new Renaissance-humanist movement, which focused on the classical art and writings of ancient Greece and Rome. Through study humanists sought moral truths about humans and their relationship to God and the universe. The young princess excelled at her studies, speaking six languages fluently at an early age and impressing those around her with her keen intelligence and surprisingly mature presence. She was a healthy and athletic child who enjoyed horseback riding, hunting, music, and dance. Elizabeth lived with her half-sister, Mary, and later with Edward in a household attended by educated noblewomen. Though Henry initially stayed away, he took increasing interest in her as she grew up. Elizabeth adored him.

After her father's death Elizabeth lived with her stepmother, Katherine Parr. Parr had quickly remarried to her former love, the Lord Admiral Thomas Seymour (1508–1549), the Duke of Somerset's brother, and soon was carrying his child. Seymour was a handsome, bold man with overpowering ambitions. He began to make inappropriate advances to the fourteen-year-old Elizabeth. The princess was intrigued by him. As rumors started to spread, Parr sent Elizabeth to live elsewhere. Shortly thereafter Parr died of complications from childbirth.

Seymour began to consider the possibility of marrying Elizabeth, but shortly into their courtship he was caught in attempting to kidnap young king Edward and take over his brother's position as regent. With Seymour in prison Edward's councilors immediately began to question Elizabeth about her involvement in his plot. Interrogations of her household attendants revealed every embarrassing detail of the flirtation with Seymour. Elizabeth, though disgraced and prohibited from visiting her brother at the royal court, maintained her innocence under severe questioning, demanding that the council put an end to the wild rumors about her that were circulating around England. Thomas Seymour, probably her first romantic interest, was beheaded for treason. Elizabeth never expressed her feelings about this incident to anyone.

For Elizabeth, as for many English people, the reign of her half-sister, Mary, was a terrifying time. Mary suspected Elizabeth of involvement in Wyatt's rebellion and had her imprisoned in the Tower of London, a fortress on the Thames River in London that was used as a royal residence, treasury, and, most famously, as a prison for the upper class, for two months. Elizabeth was interrogated repeatedly, but never wavered from protesting her complete innocence. Even so, Mary believed that as long as Elizabeth lived, she would be a threat. Although the queen seemed eager to eliminate her sister, the people of England supported the princess, who was becoming a popular figure. Finally Mary's husband, Philip II, who had become the king of Spain, interceded on Elizabeth's behalf. Philip knew that uprisings were likely to occur if the queen had her sister executed. Some historians speculate the Philip realized his wife was dying and wanted to be on good terms with her successor. At his insistence Mary released Elizabeth into the custody of a nobleman who watched her. Mary demanded that Elizabeth attend Catholic Mass and Elizabeth obeyed rather than risk being executed as a heretic. She spent the rest of Mary's reign in great fear for her life.

For More Information

BOOKS

Brigden, Susan. *New Worlds, Lost Worlds: The Rule of the Tudors, 1485–1603.* New York: Penguin Books, 2000.

Powicke, Sir Maurice. *The Reformation in England.* London: Oxford University Press, 1941.

Schama, Simon. *A History of Britain: At the Edge of the World? 3500 BC –1603 AD.* New York: Hyperion, 2000.

Smith, Lacey Baldwin. *Henry VIII: The Mask of Royalty.* London: Panther, 1971.

Tillyard, E. M. W. *The Elizabethan World Picture.* New York: Vintage Books, 1942.

WEB SITES

Knox, Ellis L. "The Reformation in England." *History of Western Civilization.* http://history.boisestate.edu/westciv/reformat/englnd01.htm (accessed on July 11, 2006).

Pettegree, Andrew. "The English Reformation." *Church and State: BBC History.* http://www.bbc.co.uk/history/state/church_reformation/ english_reformation_01.shtml (accessed on July 11, 2006).

"Tudor England." http://englishhistory.net/tudor/contents.html (accessed on July 11, 2006).

3

Elizabeth Takes the Throne

On November 17, 1558, Queen Mary I (1516–1558; reigned 1553–58) died. A messenger from the royal court in London delivered the news to Elizabeth (1533–1603), heir to the throne. According to English legend, he found her reading a Bible under an oak tree in her garden. Upon hearing of her half-sister's death, Elizabeth fell to her knees. The messenger heard her recite in Latin from Psalm 118: "This is the Lord's doing: and it is marvelous in our eyes" (as quoted in Peter Brimacombe's *All the Queen's Men: The World of Elizabeth I*). Whether or not the legend is true, it illustrates Elizabeth's belief that divine intervention had spared her life during the dark days of Mary's reign. (For more information on the reign of Mary I, see Chapter 2.) For the rest of her life, Elizabeth held an unshakable faith that it was by God's design that she was queen of England. Though only twenty-five years old and wholly unskilled in the art of governing a country, she was remarkably confident and ready to assume her role as England's supreme leader.

The challenges ahead were daunting. Mary had left the country in a weak state. Bad crops had caused famine, or the scarcity of food causing widespread hunger or starvation, and the royal treasury was without funds. England had lost its status as a major European power, and both France and Spain had grown far more powerful. Though many English people feared foreign invasion, England's worst hostilities were internal. The country had become greatly divided by the religious upheavals of the previous three reigns. It had been torn from its traditional spiritual center, the Roman Catholic Church, by Elizabeth's father, Henry VIII (1491–1547; reigned 1509–47). In 1547, under Edward VI (1537–1553; reigned 1547–53), the English people had been required to worship as Protestants. Only six years later, Mary had restored Catholicism and England's ties with the pope and the Catholic Church in Rome, and she had enforced the national religion by burning Protestants at the stake. With each change of the nation's official religion, English Catholics

WORDS TO KNOW

bishop: A clergyman with a rank higher than a priest, who has the power to ordain priests and usually presides over a diocese.

coronation: The crowning ceremony in which a monarch officially becomes king or queen.

episcopal: Governed by bishops.

famine: The scarcity of food causing widespread hunger or starvation.

heresy: A religious opinion that conflicts with the church's doctrines.

Holy Roman Empire: A loose confederation of states and territories, including the German states and most of central Europe, that existed from 962 to 1806 and was considered the supreme political body of the Christian people.

pageant: A dramatic presentation, such as a play, that often depicts a historical, biblical, or traditional event.

pious: Highly devoted to one's religion.

presbyterian: Governed by presbyters, or church elders.

Privy Council: The board of advisors that carried out the administrative function of the government in matters of economy, defense, foreign policy, and law and order, and its members served as the king's or queen's chief advisors.

progress: A royal procession, or trip, made by a monarch and a large number of his or her attendants.

Reformation: A sixteenth-century religious movement that aimed to reform the Roman Catholic Church and resulted in the establishment of Protestant churches.

regent: Someone who rules for a king or queen when the monarch is absent, too young, or unable to rule.

retinue: Group of attendants.

Tower of London: A fortress on the Thames River in London that was used as a royal residence, treasury, and, most famously, as a prison for the upper class.

transubstantiation: In Roman Catholic doctrine, the miraculous change that occurs when a priest blesses the Eucharist (bread and wine) and it changes into the body and blood of Christ, while maintaining the appearance of bread and wine.

feared for the fate of their souls and Protestants became more determined to fight for their right to worship in the manner they believed to be right. It was difficult to imagine how unity could be restored to the nation.

Getting started

By the time of her death, Mary was not a popular queen, and most of the British people hoped Elizabeth would establish a more peaceful future. Parliament (the English legislative body) happened to be in session on the day of Mary's death, and it lost no time in proclaiming Elizabeth the new queen of England. A period of two months then passed between Mary's death and Elizabeth's coronation, or crowning as queen, on January 15, 1559. Elizabeth made good use of that time.

One of her first acts was to appoint William Cecil (1520–1598; later Lord Burghley) as her secretary of state. Cecil, a Protestant, had participated in the government of Edward VI. He had stayed out of the public eye during Mary's reign and therefore escaped imprisonment and execution for heresy as a Protestant. Heresy is a religious opinion that conflicts with the church's doctrines. During this time he had quietly served the princess Elizabeth, and his qualities had impressed her greatly. Cecil was well-educated and highly experienced in governmental affairs and, perhaps more importantly, he exhibited moderation and honesty in all that he did. When Elizabeth appointed him as her chief minister, she said to him, as quoted by Peter Brimacombe: "This judgment I have of you, that you will not be corrupted with any manner of gift and that you will be faithful to the state and that without respect of my private will, you will give me that council that you think best." Like most Englishmen, Cecil did not at first believe any woman was fit to rule the country, but he worked very hard over the next forty years to serve his queen and country.

Like Elizabeth, Cecil was extremely cautious and did not like sudden changes. Because of this tendency, he often served as a balancing force in matters of state, countering the rash schemes of other advisors and courtiers with his practical, but usually conservative (tending to preserve things as they are) suggestions. From the start Cecil was Elizabeth's most trusted advisor and consequently the second most powerful person in England. Most historians believe the match between the queen and her top advisor was an extraordinarily favorable one for England. Still, the chief minister was limited in his authority. Elizabeth always asked for and listened to the advice of her councilors, but she never ceded her power to make the final decisions to anyone, including Cecil.

Once Cecil was enlisted, Elizabeth got to work selecting her Privy Council. The Privy Council was a board of advisors that carried out the administrative function of Elizabeth's government in matters of economy, defense, foreign policy, and law and order, and its members served as her chief advisors. Not all of the members were active in their duties, but the chief members, such as the secretary, the lord treasurer, the lord chamberlain, and the lord chancellor were extremely influential. Mary's Privy Council had been large, with about fifty members. Elizabeth quickly dismissed most of Mary's council, saying, as quoted in David Starkey's *Elizabeth: The Struggle for the Throne,* that "a multitude doth

Elizabeth I named William Cecil her secretary of state.
© BETTMANN/CORBIS.

make rather disorder and confusion than good council." She reduced her council to nineteen, appointing a few promising statesmen who were moderate in their religious beliefs. She did not appoint any members of the clergy.

Another vital appointment Elizabeth made during the first days of her reign was her Master of Horse, the dashing Robert Dudley (1532–1588; later Earl of Leicester). Dudley had been educated with the royal family and had known Elizabeth since she was eight years old. The two had become friends; Elizabeth had even attended Dudley's marriage to an heiress in 1550. Dudley was the son of John Dudley, Duke of

Northumberland (1501–1554), the regent who ruled England in the name of the young Edward VI. A regent is someone who rules for a king or queen when the monarch is absent, too young, or unable to rule. After Edward's death Dudley's father, Northumberland, had been responsible for the plan to place Lady Jane Grey (1537–1554) on the English throne instead of Mary, for which he was executed. (For more information on the plot to crown Jane Grey, see Chapter 2.) The younger Dudley had played a minor role in the affair, and for this he was imprisoned in the Tower of London (a fortress on the Thames River in London used as a royal residence, treasury, and, most famously, as a prison for the upper class). Elizabeth was being held in the Tower at the same time under suspicion of being involved in a conspiracy against Mary. It is not known if the two were able to communicate with each other while in prison.

Dudley was well suited to the position of Master of Horse, a job that entailed managing transportation for the queen and attending her on her rides, as well as overseeing Elizabeth's entertainment and her notorious progresses—royal processions, or trips, made by a monarch and a large number of his or her attendants. Dudley excelled in horsemanship and was an expert at putting together magnificent public events. Elizabeth liked to ride daily, and thus he spent many hours at her side. He quickly came to rival Cecil in holding the queen's trust.

The coronation ceremonies

Several days after appointing her Privy Council, Elizabeth rode into London with a retinue of more than one thousand attendants. The people of the city flocked to greet her, singing and cheering as she rode her horse ceremoniously through the streets. Elizabeth then began preparing for her coronation ceremony. Though her income was limited and the treasury of England had been depleted by years of poor management, she knew that, as a young woman in a stormy political world, she needed to make a majestic impression to awe her subjects into devotion and obedience.

On January 14, 1559, the eve of her coronation, the twenty-five-year-old queen dressed for her royal entry, or ceremonial passage into the city of London, in a robe made of gold and silver cloth trimmed in ermine (an expensive white fur) and covered in gold lace. On her head she wore, for the last time, her small crown designed for a princess. She rode in a large, open litter (a vehicle designed to be carried by attendants to transport an important person) covered in white satin and trimmed in gold

Economic Reform

One of the reasons England was in bad financial shape when Elizabeth took the throne was that its money system had been debased, or lost value. The debasement had begun during the reign of her father, Henry VIII. At the time England's money was in the form of gold and silver coins. To raise funds for the wars he was conducting in France and Scotland, Henry issued new coins made of cheaper metals but representing the same value as the gold and silver coins. Thus, for a small investment in cheap metals, he was able to produce huge quantities of money. Edward VI also resorted to this strategy for raising funds. In time people began to hoard the old gold and silver coins; many large financial institutions refused to accept the new coins. Trade with other countries became difficult, because the other countries could not rely on the value of English money. English businesses were hurt and the economy suffered.

Within a year of taking the throne, Elizabeth initiated a program to stabilize the English money. The newer, debased coins were withdrawn from circulation and melted down, and new gold and silver money was minted. Almost immediately, England gained respect in European trade and businesses began to thrive. An economic recovery followed.

brocade. She was seated on large satin cushions and covered with a white quilt to keep her warm throughout the winter afternoon. Her litter was surrounded by footmen dressed in red velvet and directly behind her rode her Master of Horse, Dudley. Following Dudley were the queen's ladies-in-waiting and her Privy Council. Behind them rode one thousand of her bejeweled and exquisitely dressed courtiers on horses outfitted in brilliant red harnesses.

During her royal entry the Londoners presented songs, poems, and gifts to the queen. Five pageants were staged for her benefit. Pageants are dramatic presentations, such as plays, that often depict a historical, biblical, or traditional event. By all the accounts Elizabeth was radiant, successfully captivating her public. She listened to every speech with attention, personally thanked every man, woman, and child who approached with a meager gift or expression of good will, and dazzled the crowds with brief speeches in which she promised to be the most loving monarch England had ever known. She emphasized two key themes: being "mere English" (avoiding foreign influences) and her preference for the English translation of the Bible. This delighted Londoners, who were largely Protestant. At least for one day Elizabeth relieved some of the discomfort that most English subjects felt about

A lord presents a gift of gloves to Elizabeth at her coronation. Many Londoners presented songs, poems, and other gifts to their new queen.
© BETTMANN/CORBIS.

being ruled by a woman. She had begun to create an almost mythical image of herself as the queen of a new age and a symbol of national pride.

The coronation ceremony the next day presented a problem for Elizabeth that foreshadowed future challenges. The English bishops, or the church leaders, were Catholic. They refused to perform the coronation ceremony with the moderate innovations Elizabeth requested. In particular the new queen wanted the prayers from the Bible to be read in both Latin (as in Catholic ceremonies) and in English (as in Protestant ceremonies), hoping to include both groups in the celebration. She did not want the priest to perform transubstantiation. (In the Catholic ceremony of transubstantiation, a priest blesses the Host or the Eucharist elements, bread and wine, and they miraculously change to become the body and blood of Christ, while maintaining the appearance of bread and wine.) One of the newer bishops finally agreed to perform the service, but even he could not stray from his religious beliefs and, against the queen's wishes, he performed the transubstantiation ceremony. The queen got up and left the room.

Elizabeth's religious settlement

In 1559 Elizabeth knew that all of England was waiting to see how she would shape the church. Determined to end the religious fears that had beset the country, Elizabeth and Cecil undertook to establish a national church for England immediately after her accession to the throne. They moved very carefully, trying not to stir anxieties in England or hostilities in Europe. Though Cecil was a Protestant, caution prevented him from moving suddenly into reforms. Elizabeth, though deeply religious, was not wholly Protestant or Catholic. Like most Protestants she refuted the authority of the pope and the Catholic transubstantiation doctrine, and she cherished the English translation of the Bible. But like most Catholics she loved the ancient traditions of the Catholic Church, preferring its stately music and art and time-honored ceremonies to the austerity (plainness) of Protestant worship. Like her father she wanted to create a church that combined some traits of both the Catholic and the Protestant form of worship. Unlike Edward and Mary she was not interested in people's private belief systems. As long as her subjects acknowledged her as the leader of the church and attended the national church, she did not care if they held Catholic or Protestant views. Elizabeth believed, as quoted by Lacey Baldwin Smith in *The Elizabethan Epic,* that there was "only one Christ Jesus and one faith: the rest is dispute about trifles." She wanted the English church to bring unity and peace to Protestants and Catholics alike in her country.

Elizabeth called her first session of Parliament to push through her religious reforms. The Anglican Church, or the Church of England, was established by two acts of Parliament in 1559. The first, the Act of Supremacy, gave the queen authority over England's church. It once again terminated England's connection with the Roman church and repealed Mary's hated heresy laws, which had made disagreeing with church doctrine a crime punishable by death. Although Parliament had accepted Henry VIII as the "supreme head" of the English church, Parliament was bitterly opposed to the idea of a woman as the head of the English church. Elizabeth therefore accepted the title of "supreme governor" of the church and agreed to leave final decisions on important church matters to its highest-ranking clergy. All clergy, agents of the crown, public officials, and graduates of the universities or the law courts were required to swear an oath to uphold the Act of Supremacy. Many of England's Catholic bishops and other clergy appointed during Mary's reign would not agree to the oath and thus were forced to leave office. Elizabeth replaced them with more moderate clergy.

Also in 1559, Parliament passed the Act of Uniformity, restoring the *Book of Common Prayer* established during Edward's reign in 1552. The *Book of Common Prayer* set out all the services, ceremonies, and rituals of the new church, so that, in effect, all of England read the same passages of the Bible, said the same prayers, and worshipped in the same way at the same time. The wording in the *Book of Common Prayer* was deliberately made vague so that both moderate Protestants and Catholics could follow their own beliefs while using it. Services of the new church were conducted in English, as opposed to the Latin that was used in Roman Catholic services, and the translated Bible with a picture of Elizabeth on its cover was readily available to all. The act made use of the book mandatory. Refusal to attend church was made punishable by a fine.

The Thirty-Nine Articles of Religion were published in 1563 to proclaim the basic truths of the new Church of England. They rejected several fundamental Catholic doctrines, such as transubstantiation and the idea that human beings can change their eternal fate through their own actions. They also affirmed several key Protestant beliefs: that the Bible was the final authority on human salvation, that salvation occurred as the result of faith in the actions of Jesus Christ, and that marriage was allowed for the church's ministers. Under Elizabeth's guidance the Thirty-Nine Articles softened some Protestant ideas, permitting certain Catholic traditions that did not conflict with the Bible. Unlike most new Protestant churches in Europe, the Anglican Church was episcopal rather than presbyterian, meaning it was run by bishops rather than by a group of elder members. The Church of England was considered to be both Catholic (though not Roman Catholic) and reformed.

Elizabeth was aware that her changes would not please either devoted Catholics or Puritans (so-named because they wished to "purify" the English church from Roman Catholicism), a new group of radical Protestants who followed John Calvin's (1509–1564) teachings. (For more information on Calvin and his philosophy, see Chapter 2.) Highly dissatisfied with Elizabeth's compromises, the Puritans wanted to form a society in which the political world conformed to the teachings of the Bible. Elizabeth was opposed to radical Catholics and Protestants alike. She believed that extremes of religion had created a harmful division between English subjects. Though few were fully satisfied with the compromises made in the church, many appreciated the peace in England. In contrast wars broke out between Catholics and Protestants in Scotland, the Netherlands, and most brutally in France.

The Virgin Queen

As soon as Elizabeth was crowned queen the English nation began to focus on the matter of her marriage. Their concern was not unwarranted. If Elizabeth died without producing an heir, it was unclear who would succeed her, that is, who would have the right to be the next king or queen. Unclear successions had historically led to civil wars, and England had had its fill of turbulence in recent years. Members of her Privy Council, including Cecil, strongly advised her to find a husband. Within a month of her coronation, Parliament petitioned the queen to marry as quickly as possible in order to provide England with a suitable heir. Elizabeth was annoyed that Parliament presumed to instruct her on such a personal matter. She coolly pointed to the ring she had received upon her coronation and proclaimed that she was already married; England was her husband and her subjects were her children. She stated, as quoted by Alison Weir in *The Life of Elizabeth*: "In the end, this shall be for me sufficient, that a marble stone shall declare that a queen, having reigned such a time, lived and died a virgin." In sixteenth-century England it was considered unnatural for a woman to remain unmarried. No one at that time dreamed the queen would stand by her words and one day become known as the Virgin Queen.

Elizabeth had many suitors. Along with being one of the most powerful women in Europe, she was young, intelligent, and attractive, with golden-red hair, piercing eyes, a tall and slim figure, and long,

Ivan the Terrible, tsar of Russia, was among the world leaders who proposed marriage to Queen Elizabeth. ©
HULTON-DEUTCSH/CORBIS.

elegant hands. Her former brother-in-law, King Philip II of Spain (1527–1598), was probably the first to ask for her hand after her accession to the throne, but soon the tsar (male king or emperor) of Russia, Ivan the Terrible (1530–1584), and King Erik of Sweden (1533–1577) also made marriage proposals. The Holy Roman Emperor, Charles V (1500–1558; the Holy Roman Emperor was a title given by the pope to the leader of the Holy Roman Empire, a loose confederation of states and territories including the German states and most of central Europe), in turn offered his sons Ferdinand and Charles, the Archduke of Austria. Elizabeth enjoyed the attention. She frequently put her foreign suitors to political use, leaving them guessing as to her intentions in order to maintain friendly relations with their countries. It is unlikely that she seriously considered marrying a foreigner after seeing how the English people had despised Mary's choice of Philip. Nor did she intend to marry a Catholic, who might destroy her religious reforms. Several English noblemen asked for Elizabeth's hand, but she did not feel they were worthy matches for a queen.

Elizabeth's subjects saw another obstacle to the queen's marriage. There was an obvious flirtation between the queen and her Master of Horse, Robert Dudley. The two were always together—on long horseback rides during the day and dancing or playing cards by night. This relationship was certainly not what the Privy Council and Parliament expected. Dudley was handsome, intelligent, and well educated, but he was not a suitable husband for the queen. He was married, his family line was not of high enough rank, and his arrogance had made him unpopular in the court. In the first year of her reign, Elizabeth did not seem to care. She showed every sign of being in love with him.

The royal court was still whispering about the queen's obvious passion for Dudley when suddenly, in 1560, Dudley's wife died in an accident in which she fell down some stairs and broke her neck. Many jumped to the conclusion that Dudley had conspired to have his wife killed so he could marry Elizabeth and become king. There were even rumors that the queen had been involved in the murder of Dudley's wife. An investigation cleared Dudley of involvement, but it was not enough. Elizabeth realized that if she married Dudley, England would always associate her with a murder plot. Her Privy Council warned her not to ruin her reputation at home and in Europe by taking such a step, and Elizabeth sorrowfully bowed to the needs of her country. Elizabeth and Dudley remained extremely close for the remaining thirty years of his life, even after Dudley infuriated the queen by secretly marrying in 1578. Elizabeth went on to have many favorites—handsome and exciting men who courted her and with whom she flirted shamelessly.

In fact Elizabeth may never have intended to marry. Her life's experiences, beginning with the disastrous romance between her mother and her father, may have made marriage seem threatening to her. Although she knew it was her duty as monarch to provide an heir to the throne, Elizabeth was more comfortable without an heir. She knew from her own experience during Mary's reign that heirs were often the focus of plots to rise up against the ruling monarch, and thus became threats. Elizabeth had been under the rigid control of others throughout her first twenty-five years and wanted no more of it. She had a will for power and did not want to share the throne or the kingdom with a husband.

The situation in Europe

Elizabeth knew upon taking the throne that she had inherited a weak nation in jeopardy of losing its independence. Compared to other nations England was poor and backward, lacking a strong military and navy, and it had no overseas empire. Though at one time England had been one of the conquering forces of Europe, by the mid-sixteenth century its significance abroad was mainly limited to its alliances with stronger nations. By far the most powerful states in Europe were Spain and France, both devotedly Catholic countries. Their wars with each other had long distracted them from the affairs of England, but the two rivals signed a peace treaty in 1559.

France

France had been severely divided by the Reformation, a sixteenth-century religious movement that aimed to reform the Roman Catholic Church and resulted in the establishment of Protestant churches. A group of Protestant reformers called Huguenots, who followed the religious doctrine of the French Protestant theologian John Calvin (see Chapter 2), fought for power and religious freedom against the Catholic French Crown. Some of France's most powerful noble families were Huguenots; these nobles provided strength and financial backing to the rapidly growing movement. The result was an era of religious warfare, in which the pious on both sides were convinced that waging war against nonbelievers was a noble cause. When Elizabeth took the throne in 1559, many English people were concerned that the French zeal for religious

Map of Europe during the reign of Elizabeth I. MAP BY XNR PRODUCTIONS. THE GALE GROUP.

warfare would extend across the channel to their island. What particularly alarmed Elizabeth about France was the "auld alliance," its ancient bond with England's neighbor to the north, Scotland. The French had troops in place in Scotland and, with Elizabeth's accession, they had begun to press their claim to the English throne.

Scotland and England had centuries of hostilities behind them, and the alliance between its two enemies was a point of perpetual concern for England. Rivalry between the English and the French over Scotland came to a head in 1542, when Scotland's King James V (1512–1542) died, leaving his only child, the seven-day-old infant Mary Stuart (often called

The French Wars of Religion (1562–98)

A group of Protestant reformers called Huguenots formed in France in the sixteenth century, supporting the ideas of the French Protestant theologian John Calvin. At the time Elizabeth took the throne of England, there were more than two thousand Huguenot churches in France. Huguenots came from all social classes and were represented among some of France's most distinguished noble families. They came to be a powerful political as well as religious faction. As the number of Huguenots grew, hostility between them and the Catholics increased. In 1562 this conflict erupted in Vassey, France; a fight between Catholics and Huguenots resulted in a massacre of an unknown number of Huguenots. (An estimated thirty to twelve hundred people were slain.) The Huguenots organized to fight back, however, and they had the determination, numbers, and resources to do so. Eight consecutive religious wars followed, devastating France for the next thirty-five years. The height of the violence against the Huguenots was the Saint Bartholomew's Day Massacre on August 24, 1572. Starting as a three-day massacre of three thousand Huguenots in Paris, the killing spread throughout France. When it was over, somewhere between thirty thousand and seventy thousand Huguenots had been killed.

Mary, Queen of Scots; 1542–1587), to succeed him. Mary had royal French blood, but as the granddaughter of Henry VIII's oldest sister, Margaret Tudor, she was also one of the most legitimate heirs to the English throne. Both France and England desperately wanted to ally themselves with Scotland through a marriage between the infant queen and one of their royal princes. Henry VIII tried to arrange a marriage between his son, Edward, and Mary, but the Scottish nobility, who detested England, rose up in protest against the marriage. Henry then began a policy called "rough wooing"—a series of bloody invasions of Scotland with the purpose of forcing the marriage. In the end France sent soldiers and money to help the badly beaten Scots fight off the English. In return for French help the Scots sent their young queen to France to be raised.

At the age of fifteen Mary Stuart married the heir to the French throne, Francis (1544–1560), cementing the auld alliance. In July 1559, when Mary's husband became King Francis II, she became the queen of France as well as Scotland. With her Tudor blood, Mary also claimed the right to the English crown on the grounds that Elizabeth was illegitimate, since the Catholic Church did not acknowledge Henry VIII's divorce from Catherine of Aragon to marry Elizabeth's mother. Francis, as he

Mary Stuart, Queen of Scots, claimed the right to the English throne. ARCHIVE PHOTOS/ GETTY IMAGES.

took the French throne, publicly denied Elizabeth's right to rule England and petitioned the pope to declare her illegitimate. However, the young king died within a year, before anything came of his challenge to Elizabeth's rule.

The Scottish Reformation

When Elizabeth took the throne of England, Scotland was ruled by a regent, Mary Stuart's mother, the French Catholic Mary of Guise. Like England, Scotland was deeply divided by the Protestant Reformation. In

1557 a large group of Calvinist Scottish nobles had signed a document renouncing Catholicism and supporting a reformed Church of Scotland. Scotland became divided. While the Scottish Catholics wished to

Protestant reformer John Knox's sermon at Perth inspired several uprisings across Scotland. HULTON ARCHIVE/ GETTY IMAGES.

maintain the auld alliance with France, the Protestant reformers supported a new alliance with England. In May 1559, in the Scottish city of Perth, Protestant religious reformer John Knox (c. 1513–1572) delivered a stirring sermon, inspiring a series of major Protestant uprisings across central Scotland. By October, the Protestant lords had ousted Mary of Guise from the regency. Shortly after she was overthrown, Mary of Guise unexpectedly died.

Suddenly finding themselves leading their country, the lords of Scotland were determined to banish English and French troops and take over their own government. Elizabeth sent Cecil to the capital city of Edinburgh to represent England in the treaty negotiations among Scotland, France, and England. Cecil demanded that France—and particularly Mary, Queen of Scots—acknowledge Elizabeth as the rightful queen of England. In exchange for this Cecil unofficially suggested that Mary might become the heir to the throne if Elizabeth died without children, provided that Mary did not marry without Elizabeth's consent.

Under the terms of the Treaty of Edinburgh (1560), both France and England withdrew their troops from Scotland. Within a month the Scottish Parliament abolished the Roman Catholic Church and established the Church (or Kirk) of Scotland, a Calvinist reformed church organized along presbyterian lines. Presbyterianism is the Calvinist form of church organization, in which a group of elders, or more experienced church members, leads the church. Scotland had become a Protestant nation. Mary, Queen of Scots, a devoted Catholic, fully French in speech and customs, returned home to rule Scotland after the death of her husband.

Spain

England and Spain had traditionally been allies. Indeed, Philip II, the king of Spain, was England's king at the time of Mary's death. Philip ruled a large empire that included present-day Spain, Italy, the Low Countries—which at that time were comprised roughly of the present-day states of the Netherlands, Belgium, Luxembourg, and small parts of northern France and Germany. Spain also ruled over large portions of the New World, as North and South America were called after their discovery in the fifteenth century. Plundering the gold and silver treasures of the Inca in Peru and the Aztecs in Mexico had made Spain extremely rich, and its navy had grown into the most powerful European fleet. Philip was a devout Catholic and a strong defender of the pope and the Roman

Catholic Church. As he aged he came to believe it was his destiny to wage wars to spread the Catholic religion throughout Europe.

Fortunately for Elizabeth, Philip had more pressing problems than England in the 1560s, especially in securing his control of the Low Countries. Many of his subjects in the Netherlands had taken up Protestant reform. Philip tried to stamp out the rising force of Protestantism, and in doing so he suppressed the political, economic, and religious liberties that had long been cherished by the Dutch people. As a result, both Roman Catholics and Protestants rebelled against him under the leadership of William the Silent, prince of Orange (1533–1584). This revolt against the Spanish set off the Eighty Years' War (1568–1648) between the Netherlands and Spain.

Philip was careful to remain on friendly terms with England, which controlled the channel of water separating it from the Netherlands. As Elizabeth took the throne, Philip was willing to overlook her tendency toward Protestant reforms, believing that she could be persuaded to return to the traditional Catholic faith. Shortly after her coronation Philip submitted a marriage proposal to the young queen, hoping to peacefully maintain his station in England and preserve its Catholic traditions while pursuing his more urgent problems in the Netherlands. Elizabeth pretended to be interested in Philip's marriage proposal and used a series of delaying tactics rather than answer him, hoping to keep Spain friendly with England as long as possible.

For More Information

BOOKS
Brigden, Susan. *New Worlds: The Rule of the Tudors, 1485–1603.* New York: Penguin Books, 2000.

Brimacombe, Peter. *All the Queen's Men: The World of Elizabeth I.* New York: St. Martin's Press, 2000.

Bryant, Arthur. *The Elizabethan Deliverance.* New York: St. Martin's Press, 1981.

Starkey, David. *Elizabeth: The Struggle for the Throne.* New York: Perennial, 2001.

Watkins, Susan, with photographs by Mark Fiennes. *In Public and in Private: Elizabeth I and Her World.* London: Thames and Hudson, 1998.

PERIODICALS
McKinnon-Bell, David. "Reduced to Cinders: The Impact of the French Religious Wars." *History Review,* September 2000, p. 12.

WEB SITES

"Elizabeth: The Religious Settlement: The Middle Way." *National Maritime Museum: Royal Observatory Greenwich.* http://www.nmm.ac.uk/server/show/conWebDoc.6129/setPaginate/No (accessed on July 11, 2006).

Thomas, Heather. "Elizabeth." http://www.elizabethi.org/us/ (accessed on July 11, 2006).

4

The Elizabethan Court

In Elizabethan England there was one center of power—the royal court. A royal court is difficult to define because it changed constantly, but it was generally made up of the queen and all of the people who clustered around her, taking care of her household and personal needs and helping her to govern the country. This was a very complex operation. Elizabeth I's (1533–1603; reigned 1558–1603) retinue, or group of attendants, ranged from one thousand to fifteen hundred people. Court members included household staff, such as cooks and bakers, and the highest statesmen in England, including the Privy Council, a powerful group of nineteen (later fourteen) advisors and administrators who carried out most of the day-to-day governing of the kingdom. At court one would usually also find many visiting dignitaries (people of high rank or importance), both foreign and English, and their attendants.

Elizabeth's court was concerned with more than governmental or domestic issues. The queen also attracted the greatest scholars, artists, explorers, scientists, and performers from England and abroad. She was enthusiastic about music, dance, literature, and drama, and she was fascinated by the tales of explorers and the mysteries being uncovered by scientists and scholars. Though she never traveled beyond southern England, she spoke six languages fluently and conversed easily with foreign dignitaries. With her great energy and intellectual curiosity, her court became the center stage in the development of the Renaissance, a cultural movement involving the rebirth of classical thinking and the arts that had been occurring in Europe for over a century. Though Elizabeth firmly believed in many rigid social structures from the past, her reign brought about a cultural revolution in England, giving rise to new views on human nature and the seemingly unlimited potential of human reason and spirit.

WORDS TO KNOW

allegory: A story or painting that represents abstract ideas or principles as characters, figures, or events.

archbishop: The head bishop of a province or district.

bishop: A clergyman with a rank higher than a priest who has the power to ordain priests and usually presides over a district called a diocese.

bureaucracy: Staff of administrative officials.

clergy: Authorized religious leaders, such as priests and ministers.

coronation: The crowning ceremony in which a monarch officially becomes king or queen.

courtier: A person who serves or participates in the royal court or household as the king's or queen's advisor, officer, or attendant.

dignitary: A person of high rank or importance.

etiquette: The conduct expected to be followed in a social or official environment.

gentry: Landowners who did not hold titles but were from influential families.

knight: A man granted a rank of honor by the monarch for his personal merit or service to the country.

lady-in-waiting: A woman in the queen's household who attends the queen.

masque: A short drama, usually full of music and dance, that presents an allegory.

nobles: Elite men and women who held social titles.

patronage system: A system in which a person with a lot of power or wealth grants favors to, financially supports, enters into contracts with, or appoints to office people who in return must promise to give their political support or access to their artistic achievements.

peer: A noble holding the title of duke, marquis, earl, viscount, or baron.

progress: A royal procession, or trip, made by a monarch and a large number of his or her attendants.

retinue: Group of attendants.

shire: County.

The powers of the queen

The English monarchy was based on the principle of the divine, or God-given, right of the monarch (king or queen) to rule the nation. Elizabeth was considered God's representative on earth; no human being in the kingdom was her equal. That meant, in theory, that no one could question her judgment or rebel against her. In reality, though, no monarch ever wielded absolute power in England. The English Crown did not have enough money to pay for a national army, police force, or a large bureaucracy (staff of administrative officials) to carry out the day-to-day administration of the kingdom. For these tasks the monarch relied on the country's upper classes—the nobility and the gentry. (Nobles were a small group of elite men and women who held social titles. The gentry were landowners who did not hold titles but were from influential families.)

Elizabeth was a gifted politician who seemed to know instinctively how to persuade or manipulate her courtiers. Courtiers were people who served or participated in the royal court or household as the king or queen's advisors, officers, or attendants. She allowed the nobles and gentry enough of a role in her government that most did not feel left out, but she remained remarkably powerful. From the start Elizabeth participated fully in all the major decisions—and many of the minor ones—of her kingdom. The members of her Privy Council were experienced statesmen. When the inexperienced, twenty-five-year-old queen took the throne, they assumed she would leave the important decision-making to them. They were wrong. Though Elizabeth listened to her advisors, in the end she made the decisions herself. She required all documents and letters on state matters to pass through her hands, even when it meant working late into the night to read and respond to them. In the early years of her reign her active participation in the government worried and frustrated her councilors. Most did not think a woman was capable of ruling the kingdom. Nevertheless, they carried out her will, and in time they learned to respect her political instincts as well as her title.

There were other governmental institutions in England outside of Elizabeth's court, the largest of which was the English Parliament. Parliament was made up of the monarch and two Houses. The House of Lords was comprised of the nobility and higher clergy, namely, bishops, or clergymen above the level of priest who preside over a district, and archbishops, bishops who oversee entire prov-inces. To sit in the House of Lords was a birthright; every peer (noble holding the title of duke, marquis, earl, viscount, or baron) in England was personally summoned to sit in the House of Lords. The House of Commons was comprised of knights (men granted a rank of honor by the monarch for their personal merit or service to the country), merchants, and other commoners who were selected as representatives by the shires, or counties, and towns of England. Part of Parliament's role in the government was to present the views of the English people to the queen. Parliament infuriated the queen, for example, when it petitioned her to marry soon after her acces-sion. The main function of Parliament in Elizabeth's time, though, was to serve the queen. It was brought together at the queen's request to enact laws or to levy taxes, usually to raise money for wars. Though monarchs could impose laws without Parliament, Parliamentary statutes—those passed by both houses of Parliament and approved by the monarch—formed the highest law of England. While English people believed in the divine right of the queen, it was the "queen in Parliament"—a combination of the royal will and the voice of the people—that was the final authority.

Other governmental organizations carried out England's business and legal functions. The Exchequer was the center of finance and accounting. There was a central court system in Westminster Palace in London. Twice yearly its judges traveled to the remote regions of England to check up on local law enforcement and administration. Elizabethan England had fifty-three shires. The gentry in each shire enforced the royal laws and regulations. Local law and order was overseen by the country's fifteen hundred justices of the peace, who were assisted by sheriffs, or law enforcers. The two most distant regions of England, Wales and the northern shires, each had their own Regional Councils, which were powerful Crown-appointed assemblies headed by a Lord President. The royal court, however, was the final authority over all governmental institutions in England.

The queen's revenue

For her day-to-day expenses Elizabeth relied on her personal income, which was estimated to be about £250,000 per year in 1558, and about £600,000 per year at the time of her death. The largest part of her revenue came from renting out the sixty royal estates she had inherited. She also received income from court fines and fees and from special taxes. Although her annual income amounted to a lot of money at that time—enough to keep up her palaces and feed her huge retinue—it was not sufficient to cover major expenses, such as the high cost of war or the creation of a navy. For these Elizabeth had to convene, or call together, Parliament and ask for taxes to be imposed on the English people. Calling a Parliamentary session was always a last resort. Taxation was very unpopular, and Elizabeth was usually reluctant to convene Parliament, since it nearly always meant sharing power in some way.

Elizabeth was good at managing money, particularly in the first half of her reign. In fact some considered her to be too frugal. Her desire to save money caused her to consistently resist going to war. Though most historians today view this as a positive factor in bringing peace and stability to England, at the time Elizabeth's council members often lamented her reluctance to engage in the turbulent religious wars in Europe.

Palaces and homes

Elizabeth had many royal palaces at her disposal. She traveled regularly among several residences that were each large enough to accommodate her one thousand attendants. The royal court most often resided at the Palace of Whitehall, the largest palace in Europe, with over fifteen hundred rooms. Whitehall occupied about twenty-five acres in the

Elizabeth traveled between several residences, but the palace at Greenwich was one of her favorites. HULTON ARCHIVE/GETTY IMAGES.

heart of London and had long been the center of the English government and the main residence of the monarch. It had what was considered to be the finest art collection in England, with great paintings, statues, and tapestries from all over the world lining its walls and galleries. One of Elizabeth's favorite abodes was the palace in which she was born, Greenwich. Greenwich faced the Thames River in what is now suburban London. At Greenwich the queen kept her royal barge (a large, flat-bottomed boat), using it to travel up and down the river with twenty men at the oars. Richmond Palace, the residence Elizabeth called her "warm box," in which she liked to spend her winters, was west of London. She also stayed at Hampton Court, an eight-hundred-room palace with extensive gardens in which she enjoyed walking. Another regular residence was Windsor Castle, perched high over the Thames River west of London. After housing English royalty for over nine hundred years, Windsor remains an official residence of England's monarchy and is the largest occupied castle in the world. Later in her reign Elizabeth would acquire a country palace built by her father, Henry VIII (1491–1547), called Nonsuch, in the southeastern county of Surrey. Of all the palaces Nonsuch was the finest example of Tudor architecture.

The queen never stayed more than a couple of months at any one palace. The court was forced to move regularly because there were no flush toilets or plumbing systems. With so many people living in one place, after a time the palace and the area surrounding it began to smell. In addition local supplies for feeding and housing so many people often ran out after a prolonged stay.

Life at court

The royal court was a place where upper-class English people could achieve privileges or advancement. Most of the opportunities in the kingdom were controlled by Elizabeth under a patronage system. In a patronage system a person with power or wealth grants favors to, financially supports, enters into contracts with, or appoints people who in return must pledge their political support or perform their art in court. A courtier had to be in the good graces of the queen to receive a court or government job, a monopoly (the exclusive right to sell or trade a particular good), a pension, or a knighthood.

It was very difficult for a newcomer to the royal court to attract the queen's attention. She was constantly surrounded by guards and by a group of elite courtiers already in her favor. Only gentry or peers were

The Social Ranks of Peers

The social world of Elizabethan England was hierarchical; that is, everyone had a specific level, even the nobility. The top social level in England was the queen. Directly beneath her was a very small group of titled nobility called peers. The titles of the peers were determined by their birth or created by the monarch. Elizabeth was reluctant to bestow titles, keeping the peerage numbers low. There were about fifty-seven peers in England when Elizabeth became queen, and there were never more than sixty during her reign. The titles of peers, in descending order, were:

- Duke and Duchess;
- Marquis and Marchioness;
- Earl and Countess;
- Viscount and Viscountess;
- Baron and Baroness.

Religious leaders were given peer status in England. Bishops were ranked on the level of earls, while archbishops were ranked on the level of dukes.

Dukedom, the top title of the nobility, had once been reserved only for royal princes (sons of a king), but by Elizabethan times the title was used for a few other top nobles. There was only one duke in England during Elizabeth's reign, the Duke of Norfolk, and he was executed in 1572.

Women of noble families took their titles from their husbands, if married, and from their fathers, if single. It was correct to call any male of the peerage "Lord," and any woman "My lady." Most of the peers went by a territorial title. For example, Robert Dudley, after being created earl, was the Earl of Leicester.

allowed to attend the court, and they were only allowed in the Presence Chamber, a great hall where the queen entertained and communicated with the public. Even a courtier from a well-known noble family would often wait in the halls of the Presence Chamber for months at a time without gaining the queen's notice. In the meantime, many of these hopefuls lived beyond their means, dressing in the latest fashions daily. Most sought the help of one of the favored courtiers, often offering a substantial bribe for introducing them to the queen. Even with bribery and the finest of clothing, there was no assurance of success.

Elizabeth spent much of her time in the well-guarded set of rooms of her court called the Privy Chamber. There she conducted business, entertained herself, slept, and ate. Only a few privileged attendants or courtiers could enter the Privy Chamber. Looking after Elizabeth in her private quarters were four Ladies of the Bedchamber, eight Gentlewomen of the Privy Chamber, and about six maids of honor, who served the queen her food and helped her dress. They were educated women, skilled in the same pastimes as the queen, and served as companions as well as attendants. The highly valued ladies-in-waiting positions were usually given to the daughters of the highest noble families. The young women were required to live at court and rarely received permission to leave, because the queen did not like change. In serving the demanding queen they earned every bit of the income they were paid, but most were happy to be at court. In return for good service these young women could expect Elizabeth to arrange excellent marriages for them.

The queen's favorites

Outside of the Privy Chamber, Elizabeth preferred the company of men to women. She had many favorites, the handsome and bold young men who received most of her attention. The queen enjoyed men who could challenge her intellect, and she preferred them to be handsome and confident. Most of Elizabeth's favorites were able flatterers, as well as good dancers, dressers, or horsemen. Aside from Robert Dudley (Earl of Leicester; 1532–1588), her constant companion in her first years as queen and friend for forty years, some other favorites were Christopher Hatton (1540–1591), Walter Raleigh (sometimes spelled Ralegh; c. 1552–1618), and Robert Devereux (Earl of Essex; 1566–1601). Hatton caught the queen's attention by dancing very skillfully in a court performance, but he rose in her esteem over the years and received many major appointments, including a high position on the Privy Council. Hatton was said to be so in love with Elizabeth that he never married, and there was jealous rivalry between him and Raleigh. Raleigh, an explorer and poet, came to court a bit later in the queen's reign, bringing tales of high sea adventure that fascinated her. Legend had it that, in a supremely gentlemanly act, he spread his costly cloak over a puddle so Elizabeth could cross without damaging her shoes or gown. Elizabeth knighted him, gave him estates in Ireland, and appointed him captain of her guards. Devereux was the stepson of Dudley, becoming a favorite in the queen's older years. Theirs was a turbulent relationship that ended in disaster.

Attending Elizabeth in her court was not easy. She expected a great deal of time and loyalty from her council, attendants, and favorites. She preferred not to have her courtiers' wives at court and rarely allowed her attendants to leave, making family life nearly impossible for them. Elizabeth was extremely vain about her looks, even as she grew older. Males who wished her favor paid court to her as though they were in love with her. She had a fiery temper, and did not spare her sharp tongue when annoyed. She once threw a shoe at a courtier in a temper tantrum, and on

According to legend, Sir Walter Raleigh once cast his cloak over a puddle so that Elizabeth could cross over it without damaging her shoes or gown. © CHRIS HELLIER/CORBIS.

another occasion she boxed a courtier's ears. She shocked some of her intimates with her colorful swearing. But the queen also showed warm and loyal affection to her closest associates. Most of her courtiers were genuinely drawn to her magnetic presence, and to them she was known as the "sun queen." Her godson, the courtier and writer John Harington (1560–1612) summarized, as quoted in Neville Williams's essay "The Tudors": "When she smiled, it was a pure sunshine that everyone did choose to bask in if they could." On the other hand, Harington added, when Elizabeth was crossed, "the thunder fell on all alike."

Elizabeth was careful never to let herself become anyone else's equal, and kept her innermost feelings to herself. Like all British monarchs she considered herself to have two bodies, the private body of a woman and the public body of a monarch. She prided herself in devoting herself to her public role, the body of the "prince" of England, as she often called herself, no matter what her private needs as a human woman were.

Keeping up appearances

Though Elizabeth was frugal in her household budget, she maintained a magnificent and hospitable court. She knew the importance of displaying the Crown's power and wealth, giving notice to all who entered her court that England and its queen were forces to be reckoned with. Although Elizabeth was too worried about expense to build new palaces, she furnished those she owned lavishly with gold and silver décor, lining the walls with fine paintings and tapestries. The queen's guests at court were received with generous hospitality, including elegant feasts and entertainment. Room and board was provided for their personal attendants.

As one might expect, the court practiced strict etiquette and great ceremony in the presence of the queen. (Etiquette is the conduct expected to be followed in a social or official environment.) When Elizabeth arrived in the Presence Chamber, her guards lined the pathway before her and trumpets sounded a fanfare to announce her arrival. It was customary for her courtiers to kneel as she walked into the room and when she addressed them. It was improper to turn one's back to the queen; to leave her presence, one had to walk out of the room backwards.

Her interest in appearances extended to her courtiers. All who attended the court were expected to dress in the latest fashion. Elizabeth herself dressed extravagantly. She was said to have about three thousand dresses in her wardrobe. Her outfits were made from the finest materials, embroidered in silver and gold, and bejeweled with precious stones. They came in many layers and pieces: the elaborate ruff, a large, stiff circular collar of made of delicate lace at the neck; the stomacher, an embroidered or jewel-studded panel worn over the chest and stomach; the kirtle, or underskirt; the farthingale, a large and stiff hooped petticoat; and a gown of the latest European fashions draped over them. It took Elizabeth's ladies-in-waiting two hours daily to dress her and don her jewels. As queen Elizabeth believed that she must be dressed more magnificently than any other woman in the country. In fact on at least one occasion she forbid one of her ladies-in-waiting to wear an especially elaborate dress that might compete with the queen's attire.

The center of English culture

Along with statesmen and representatives of foreign kings and queens, the best-known musicians, artists, philosophers, and explorers were found at court. They all sought the patronage, or support, of Elizabeth or the other nobles found at court. Playing for the court was a certain path to a successful career.

Elizabeth loved music and excelled at playing several instruments. She was an accomplished dancer, and kept her own orchestra at court so that she could dance morning and night. Well into her sixties she was frequently seen on the dance floor executing the leaps and twists of the intricate court dances, such as the volte, the pavane, and the galliard.

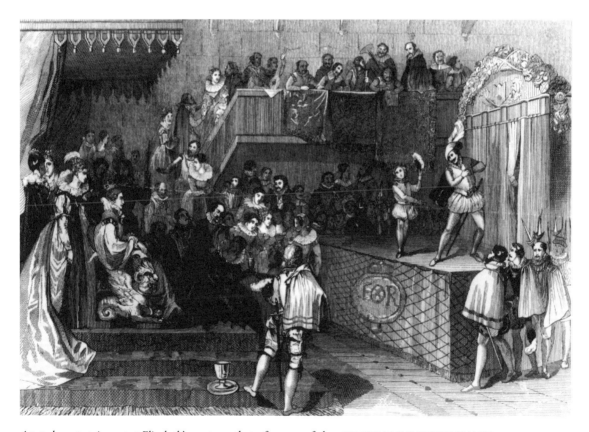

A popular entertainment at Elizabeth's court was the performance of plays. HULTON ARCHIVE/GETTY IMAGES.

Artists at court were hired to paint things in their ideal state—as the queen wished the country to see them and not the way they actually were. Thus the queen looked young and radiant in portraits even in the years after her golden hair had thinned from age and she wore thick white powder to cover her wrinkles.

The major artistic advances of Elizabethan times were made in literature and drama. Poetry was popular among the courtiers, and Elizabeth herself wrote poems. One of England's most promising young poets, Sir Philip Sidney (1554–1596), the nephew of the Earl of Leicester, was considered the ideal Elizabethan courtier. Edmund Spenser (1552–1599), author of *The Faerie Queene,* was one of the foremost poets of his age. Spenser embodied Renaissance ideals and his work reflected his strong patriotism and loyalty to his queen, who appears as "Gloriana," the symbol of English glory, in his epic poem. Walter Raleigh, too, was a noted poet and writer.

Elizabeth loved drama, and her reign will forever be associated with it. In the early years of her rule professional theaters had not yet been established. Acting companies wandered from town to town, performing medieval masques and pageants. (Masques are short dramas, full of music and dance, that present allegorical tales, stories in which characters usually represent an abstract idea, such as Death, Time, or Evil, or a historical figure, such as Elizabeth herself. Pageants are shows that usually included music and presented an idea or theme.) Acting troops were considered vagabonds and were often thrown out of towns. Many acting companies in the mid-sixteenth century began to seek the patronage of noble families. The first theater in Elizabeth's court was performed by amateur nobles, who staged masques and pageants to please the queen. Then, in the 1570s, Elizabeth's master of revels, a deputy to the Lord Chamberlain who was in charge of entertainment at court, hired professional companies to perform for Elizabeth. Soon every theater company strove to perform at the royal court. During the course of Elizabeth's reign, playwriting advanced to a highly sophisticated form, involving developed characters and plots. In the later years of her reign, the plays of England's most famous writer, William Shakespeare (1564–1616), were performed at court.

The queen's progresses

During the summer months of most years of her reign Elizabeth arranged to go on progresses, tours of the kingdom made with some portion of her court. The route of the queen's travels and every stop she was to make

Elizabeth I traveling on a litter, accompanied by her retinue. THE GRANGER COLLECTION, NEW YORK.

were prearranged well ahead of the trip. Elizabeth traveled on horseback, in a litter, or in her royal coach, usually with a retinue of about five hundred people. The trips were exhausting for most of her attendants. Planning and packing presented enormous challenges. The procession following the queen consisted of about 2,400 horses, and there were between 400 and 600 carts filled with clothing, jewelry, documents, and many household items belonging to the queen and her attendants. Travel was not easy either; the roads in England were very poor in Elizabethan times. The progress usually advanced only about ten miles a day, and the carts often got stuck. But even on the bumpy, muddy roads, Elizabeth was in her element, extending herself out to her subjects. Each time the progress crossed the border of a shire Elizabeth was welcomed by the local gentry and bells rang to announce her presence. All along the way humble farmers and working families greeted her with their good wishes and gifts, and Elizabeth showered them with her regal attention.

The main destination of a progress was usually the large country estate of a noble family selected for the honor of a visit by the queen and her advisors. For the noble families who served as her hosts Elizabeth's visits were a mixed blessing. Although it was a great honor to have such an exalted visitor, it cost a fortune to feed and house her entire retinue. There were many other expenses, even in a short stay. The queen expected to be entertained by her hosts, and wherever she went she was treated to masques, concerts, banquets, fireworks, and festivals. Many noble families tried to outdo one another in lavish hospitality and expensive gifts for the queen. Some nobility built huge country homes specifically designed to be able to accommodate the queen on one of her progresses. But other families fled their homes when they learned of an intended visit, fearing financial ruin. Indeed, Elizabeth viewed her progresses as a way to save the royal income by passing off the expense of keeping her staff and entertainment to her host.

Elizabeth enjoyed her progresses as vacations from the normal routines, but more importantly, she used them as a means to be visible to, and win the hearts of, her subjects outside the capital city of London. She usually had pamphlets describing her progresses printed and distributed throughout her realm. These depicted the splendor of the queen's procession, the adoration of the crowds who received her, and they were particularly designed to promote the mystique of the Virgin Queen. Elizabeth knew, probably through the examples of the reigns of her father, half-brother, and half-sister, that in order to maintain social stability a monarch should be visible and available to her people. Unlike her siblings, she had an instinctive understanding of people and valued spending time with her subjects. On the eve of her coronation, or crowning as queen, she told the crowds in London, as quoted from "The Receiving of the Queen's Majesty": "Be ye ensured that I will be as good unto you as ever a Queen was to her people." During her reign, Elizabeth made twenty-five progresses, much to the delight of the people of the counties through which she passed.

The new era

Elizabeth's concept of the queen's place in the universe was based on the medieval concept of the Great Chain of Being. The Great Chain can be envisioned as a huge ladder mounting up to the heavens. At the very top is God, and below God, in descending order, are the various levels of angels, the stars, the Sun, the Moon, and the planets, humans, animals, plants, and finally rocks and soil. Each element in the universe took a specific place within the hierarchy, or ranking system, according to its unchanging standing in the universe. Like the people of medieval times, Elizabeth firmly believed she was stationed at the very top of the human realm, making her part human, part divine. She believed that people should live the lives they were born into and show respect to people who were born to a higher rank. During Elizabeth's lifetime, though, popular belief in the Great Chain model was just beginning to crumble. A new middle class had arisen, and merchants were rising in the ranks of English society. Renaissance philosophers and artists portrayed human beings as capable of overcoming obstacles and conquering their environments despite the status of their birth. Though she resisted the changes in social order, Elizabeth was fascinated by the new culture, and her court attracted the bold and rash young men who were challenging the old ways.

For More Information

BOOKS

"Receiving of the Queen's Majesty." *The Queen's Majesty's Passage and Related Documents.* Germaine Warkentin, ed. Toronto: Centre for Reformation and Renaissance Studies, 2004.

Rowse, A. L. *The England of Elizabeth: The Structure of Society.* New York: Macmillan, 1961.

Watkins, Susan, with photographs by Mark Fiennes. *In Public and in Private: Elizabeth I and Her World.* London: Thames and Hudson, 1998.

Weir, Allison. *The Life of Elizabeth I.* New York: Ballantine Books, 1998.

Williams, Neville. "The Tudors." In *The Courts of Europe: Politics, Patronage, and Royalty, 1400–1800.* New York: McGraw-Hill, 1977.

PERIODICALS

Sim, Alison. "The Royal Court and Progresses." *History Today,* May 2003, Vol. 53, Issue 5.

WEB SITES

"The Hierarchy of the Elizabethan Court." *Internet Shakespeare Editions, 1998–2003.* University of Victoria. http://ise.uvic.ca/Library/SLT/history/government.html (accessed on July 11, 2006).

Somerville, J. P. "Elizabethan Government." http://history.wisc.edu/sommerville/361/361-15.htm (accessed on July 11, 2006).

5

The Catholic Reformation and Conspiracies Against Elizabeth, 1558–1580

The Roman Catholic Church had undergone many periods of change before the time of the Protestant Reformation, the sixteenth-century religious movement that resulted in the establishment of Protestant churches. But in the 1520s Catholic leaders became concerned because many of their members were leaving the church to join the Protestant movement. In an attempt to keep people from leaving the church, they tried to eliminate corruption within the church and to clarify the church's doctrine. (Doctrine is a principle, or set of principles, held by a religious or philosophical group.) Church leaders also opposed the new Protestant beliefs, which they considered heresy, or religious opinions that conflict with the church's doctrines. During this time the Catholic Church tried to reunify Europe under Catholicism and to spread Roman Catholic Christianity to the New World, Asia, and Africa. Some scholars call this period the Counter Reformation, assuming the Catholic Church was responding to the Protestant movement; most Catholics, however, refer to it as the Catholic Reformation, arguing that the effort was an independent action within the church.

When Elizabeth I (1533–1603), a Protestant, became queen of England in 1558, Catholics made up the majority of the population. Though most English Catholics remained loyal to the queen despite their religious differences, many of her chief councilors feared a Catholic uprising. Moreover, they feared that Catholic countries and societies abroad would either aid the English Catholics in a rebellion or invade England themselves in their efforts to eliminate Protestantism. There was some basis for these fears. There were English Catholics both in England and in exile in Europe who plotted to restore Catholicism in England. There were also powerful monarchs in Europe seeking to spread Catholicism. Furthermore, by the end of the 1560s, the beautiful and persuasive, exiled queen of the Scots, Mary Stuart (1542–1587), became a representative of their cause.

WORDS TO KNOW

archbishop: The head bishop of a province or district.

bishop: A clergyman ranked higher than a priest who has the power to ordain priests and usually presides over a diocese, or church district.

bull: A written communication from the pope to all Catholics worldwide.

cardinal: A top official in the Roman Catholic Church, ranking just below the pope.

clergy: Authorized religious leaders, such as priests and ministers.

Counter Reformation: Also called the Catholic Reformation; the period beginning in the 1520s when the Catholic Church, partially in response to the rise of Protestantism, tried to reunify Europe under Catholicism and to spread Roman Catholic Christianity to the New World, Asia, and Africa.

courtier: A person who serves or participates in the royal court or household as the king's or queen's advisor, officer, or attendant.

doctrine: A principle (or set of principles) held by a religious or philosophical group.

heresy: A religious opinion that conflicts with the church's doctrines.

lay person: A person who is not a member of the clergy.

missionary: A person sent by his or her church to help people of other countries and to convert nonbelievers to the church's doctrines.

papal legate: A representative of the pope within a particular nation.

Protestant Reformation: Also known as the Reformation; a sixteenth-century religious movement that aimed to reform the Roman Catholic Church and resulted in the establishment of Protestant churches.

ritual: An established ceremony performed in precise ways according to the rules of the church.

saint: A deceased person who, due to his or her exceptionally good behavior during life, receives the official blessing of the church and is believed to be capable of interceding with God to protect people on earth.

salvation: In Christianity, deliverance from sin and punishment.

seminary: A school similar to a university that trains students in religion, usually to prepare them to become members of the clergy.

The Jesuits

A new order of Catholic priests called the Jesuits, or the Society of Jesus, provided strong support to the Catholic Reformation. They were founded in 1540 by a former Spanish soldier, Ignatius of Loyola (1491–1556). Loyola had never been a particularly religious man, but after being seriously injured in battle, he suddenly became passionately Catholic. During his recuperation, Loyola had been profoundly moved when he read a book about the lives of the saints. A saint is a deceased person who receives official recognition from the church for his or her holiness during life; saints were considered capable of performing miracles and of interceding with God on behalf of the people who pray to them. Loyola wanted to follow in their footsteps and become a "soldier of God." He established the Society of Jesus to restore Catholicism to its status as the single greatest spiritual and political power in Europe and the one true religion worldwide. Known for their military-like organization, the Jesuits believed that the ends justified the means, and they were willing to resort to extreme tactics if it would benefit the church and spread the Catholic religion.

Ignatius of Loyola founded the Society of Jesus, also known as the Jesuits. NEW YORK PUBLIC LIBRARY PICTURE COLLECTION.

By the time Elizabeth became queen, the Jesuits had headquarters in nearly all the major cities of Europe. They had also established seminaries, or schools similar to a university that train students to become members of the clergy, that were training highly disciplined Jesuit missionaries. (Missionaries are people sent by the church to help people of other countries and to convert nonbelievers to the church's doctrines.) The Jesuit order did not retreat from worldly affairs. Rather, Jesuit priests were active in politics and worked to gain the trust of powerful people, including most of the Catholic monarchs of Europe. The Jesuit order also sent missionaries to the Americas, Asia, and Africa to spread Catholicism. Jesuits were also responsible for some of the Catholic Church's most charitable reforms. They created the world's first organizations designed to promote widespread social welfare: feeding the hungry, providing jobs for the unemployed, and helping the sick and elderly. This kind of charitable work had never been carried out on such a large and organized scale before.

The Council of Trent

In the 1540s the Catholic Church called all of its bishops together to discuss church reform and define Catholic beliefs. The Council of Trent first met in 1545. It would continue to meet off and on for nearly eighteen years. The Council of Trent defined Catholic beliefs in a way that clearly separated the Catholic Church from the Protestant Church. The Council ruled that the Latin Vulgate (the official Latin translation of the Bible) was the official Bible of the church, and that Latin was the language of all Catholic prayer. Protestants, on the other hand, favored the use of the Bible translated into their vernacular, or everyday, languages. The council also ruled that the ancient traditions of the Church were equal in authority to the Bible. The German Protestant leader Martin Luther (1483–1546) had, in contrast, asserted that the Bible should be the only rule of faith. The council reaffirmed the Catholic belief that the church was the only route to salvation, or deliverance from sin and punishment, and that it was the church's role to interpret and instruct its members about the Bible. The Catholic Church did not support Biblical teachings by the lay people that formed the foundation of Protestantism. (Lay people are people who are not members of the clergy.) The Council of Trent affirmed the belief that human beings could help ensure their own salvation by engaging in good work. But Protestants believed that an individual's fate is determined by God. If

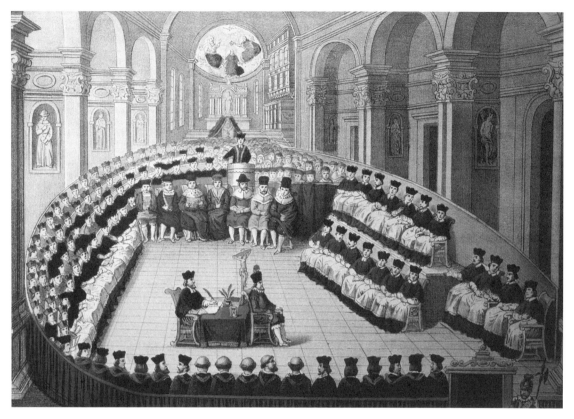

A meeting of the Council of Trent. The Council met several times over a period of eighteen years. © ARCHIVO ICONOGRAFICO, S.A./CORBIS.

God had determined that a person's soul would be sent to hell after death, no amount of good works could change that. The rulings of the Council of Trent were the most specific description of Catholic beliefs ever stated. This clearly expressed doctrine helped Catholic officials determine what was heresy and what was not.

The Catholic Queen of Scots

To Elizabeth and her advisors, the forces of the Catholic Reformation were a great threat to the security of England. Their fears increased with the return from France of Elizabeth's Catholic cousin, Mary Stuart, Queen of Scots. (For more information on Mary Stuart, see Chapters 3 and 7.) England had reason to fear her intentions. When Queen Mary I (1516–1558) had died in 1558, Mary Stuart claimed to be the heir to the English throne. Her family background supported this: she was the

The Spanish Inquisition

Spain was a major center of the Catholic Reformation during the Elizabethan Era, the period associated with the reign of Queen Elizabeth I (1558–1603) that is often considered to be a golden age in English history. This was in part because of the nation's religious experiences during the previous century. Until the late fifteenth century, Spain had been a confederation of smaller states, some of which had long been ruled by the Moors, a Muslim group. The Moorish states also contained a large Jewish population. In their struggle to conquer the Moors' territory and unify Spain, Catholic monarchs Ferdinand (1452–1516) and Isabella (1451–1504) established an inquisition in 1478. The inquisition was a Roman Catholic Church practice in which the church appointed priests to form tribunals (judicial proceedings with people appointed to act as judges) to find and eliminate heretics. (Heretics are people who do not conform to the church's beliefs).

In 1492 a newly united Spain expelled Jews and Muslims from its borders. With fewer non-Catholics in Spain, the inquisition reduced its efforts, but the tribunals remained. In the 1520s, when the Protestant Reformation spread across Europe, the Spanish Inquisition tribunals worked to combat Protestantism. In Spain, Italy, and Portugal, tribunals headed by powerful priests descended upon towns suspected of harboring heretics. Local preachers instructed their church members either to voluntarily confess to heresy or to name other suspects from the community for the inquisitors. Treatment of the accused became increasingly harsh: their land and goods were taken from them; suspected heretics were jailed at their own expense until the hearing was completed; and if the accused did not confess despite insufficient evidence, the inquisitors were permitted to use torture. Torture was not used as frequently as some historians have suggested, however.

When Elizabeth I became queen of England in 1558, the Spanish Inquisition was mainly directed against Lutherans, the followers of Protestant leader Martin Luther. Philip II (1527–1598), king of Spain and ruler of the territories in the Netherlands, was a very serious, powerful leader and a devoted Roman Catholic who felt it was his duty to fight heresy and spread the true religion. No significant Protestant movement ever became established in Spain, but Philip set the Spanish Inquisition in motion in the Netherlands to suppress Protestantism there.

great-granddaughter of Elizabeth's grandfather, King Henry VII (1457–1509). Since Elizabeth had been declared illegitimate by the Catholic Church, which did not accept the marriage between her mother, Anne Boleyn (c. 1504–1536), and her father, Henry VIII (1498–1547), Mary was, from a Catholic point of view, the logical heir to the throne.

On April 19, 1561, the nineteen-year-old Mary arrived back on Scottish shores after having lived in the French royal court for thirteen years. She had even been the French queen for one year before the untimely death of her husband, King Francis II (1544–1560). In the year before Mary's return, Protestantism had become the public religion of Scotland. Many believed that Mary, a devout Catholic, meant to reestablish the old religion and realign Scotland with Catholic states in Europe. But converting Scotland was probably never Mary's intention. In the nearly seven years she served as the queen of Scotland, she accepted Protestantism as the religion of the country, though she continued to practice Catholicism in private.

During her time in France Mary had matured into a warm, lively, and beautiful woman of nearly six feet tall. She had been well educated in the French court and had an appealing personality. Most who served her were passionately devoted to her. Her attraction was magnetic, and she was well known for being able to charm men into dangerous actions. When it came to her personal relationships, though, her judgment was questionable, causing many problems later in her life.

Both Scotland and England anxiously waited for Mary Stuart to marry, wondering what the nationality and religion of the new king might be. In July 1565 the queen of Scots married her nineteen-year-old cousin, Henry Stewart, Lord Darnley (1545–1567), with whom she claimed to have fallen deeply in love. Because Stewart was also an heir to the English throne, this marriage strengthened Mary's claims to the throne of England. Mary and Stewart had an extravagant Catholic wedding, provoking fears among the Protestant lords that they intended to bring back Catholicism to Scotland. Stewart was detested among the Scottish lords; he was immature, arrogant, lacking in morals, and by most accounts, not very smart. Soon after the wedding, the Scottish lords staged a rebellion. Mary was forced to use military force to defeat them, but she was already beginning to understand their dislike for her husband. As she grew familiar with Stewart's many faults, Mary decided not to grant him the royal powers of a king. She turned for comfort to her Italian secretary, David Rizzio (c. 1533–1566). In 1566 a jealous Stewart and a few other nobles dragged Rizzio from Mary's room and stabbed him to death.

Three months later Mary gave birth to a son, James (1566–1625; later James VI of Scotland and James I of England). The queen made an outward show of reconciliation with Stewart. Then, early in 1567, the house Stewart was staying at was destroyed in a violent explosion. He was found dead in the garden outside, apparently strangled when trying to escape. Evidence pointed to James Hepburn (Earl of Bothwell; 1535–1578) as Stewart's murderer, and many suspected that Mary was

David Rizzio, Mary Stuart's private secretary, was murdered in 1566. Mary's husband, jealous of Rizzio's relationship with the queen, and several other nobles stabbed Rizzio to death. HULTON ARCHIVE/ GETTY IMAGES.

involved. The queen would not allow an extensive investigation into the murder, and Hepburn was released after a superficial inquiry. After the investigation he was granted a divorce from his wife, and he quickly married the queen of Scots. The Scottish lords thought Mary's behavior proved her involvement in the murder. Outraged by their queen's behavior, they rebelled in 1567. This time they were successful. A defeated Mary was captured and brought into the Scottish city of Edinburgh. As she passed through the streets of the city she was insulted by the crowds, who shouted "Burn the whore." Mary Stuart was imprisoned and forced to abdicate, or give up the throne in favor of her infant son, James.

Less than a year later Mary escaped her Scottish prison. She tried to rally enough forces to take back her rule of Scotland but failed. She then attempted to flee to France, but did not receive French help and never made it out of Scotland. Finally in May 1568 Mary crossed the border into England, where she asked Elizabeth to help restore her to her kingdom. Elizabeth was torn. She was appalled that Mary, a legitimate monarch, had been treated so poorly by her subjects, but she was equally shocked at Mary's behavior and not at all happy about having the Catholic with claims to the English throne so close at hand. The rebel leaders in Scotland quickly informed her that they did not want their queen back under any circumstances. For lack of alternatives, Elizabeth set up a commission of inquiry to investigate Mary's involvement in the death of Stewart, although she herself firmly believed that no commission had the right to put a queen on trial. In the end Elizabeth would not allow the commission to make a judgment on the issue of Mary's guilt, deciding that Mary should remain in England so that the Protestant government in Scotland would be undisturbed by its scandalous queen.

Mary was placed under house arrest in the homes of noblemen who were loyal to Elizabeth. She remained an English prisoner for nearly eighteen years, from 1569 to 1587. Mary never stopped appealing to those who might have reason to help her—Catholics in Rome, Spain, and France, and those who remained in England. But her interest had turned from regaining the Scottish crown to taking the English crown. She lured potential rescuers with the promise that, with a little help from outside, she could make England a Catholic nation once more.

Plots against Elizabeth

Plots against Elizabeth began soon after Mary arrived in England. The chairman of the commission that had tried Mary, Thomas Howard, Duke of Norfolk (1536–1572), was one of Elizabeth's closest advisors and the highest ranking noble in England. He had been disgusted by the overwhelming evidence of adultery and murder presented against Mary. Yet despite his disgust, Howard was unable to resist either her charms or his own ambitions. He soon began to consider the idea of marrying the queen of Scots. At first many of Elizabeth's councilors supported the plan, thinking Howard could keep the Scottish queen under careful control. But when Elizabeth heard of the plan she was suspicious, and summoned Howard to appear at court. Guilty and fearing the queen's anger, Howard repeatedly claimed illness as the reason for staying away from court. He and Mary were in constant communication and planning their marriage.

The Northern Rising and the papal bull

Even as she made plans with Howard, the queen of Scots was at the center of another plot in northern England. The shires, or counties, in the north had always been so remote from the capital in southern England that the powerful noble families ruled their districts almost independently of the queen. Protestantism had never thrived in the north, and even after Elizabeth established the Anglican Church as the official, Protestant

English nobleman Thomas Howard was involved in one of the many plots against Elizabeth. © BETTMANN/ CORBIS.

church of the nation, the northern nobles continued to practice Catholicism in defiance of the laws of the land. They resented the new Protestant queen and in 1568 began to plot a rebellion to overthrow Elizabeth and place Mary on the English throne. The plot was communicated abroad with the help of the Spanish ambassador to England, and the lords were put in touch with a banker from Florence (in present-day Italy), named Roberto Ridolfi (1531–1612) and the French king, both of whom promised to provide financial support. Through spies, though, Elizabeth heard about the preparations for the uprising. She feared that

Howard might join the rebellion, and he was arrested and held in the Tower of London.

In November 1569 the northern lords gathered twenty-five hundred men and marched south toward Tutbury in a rebellion called the Northern Rising. They headed straight for the residence of Mary Stuart with the intention of releasing her and claiming her as their queen. Under Elizabeth's orders Mary was moved so the rebels could not get to her. By December the rebellion had collapsed. The queen's forces chased the rebels back to the north. Though many of the nobles were able to flee from England, hundreds of their troops were brutally executed. The powerful noble families lost their land and titles. Without land and titles, they no longer had enough power and influence to be a threat to Elizabeth.

The head of the Roman Catholic Church, Pope Pius V (1504–1572), wanted to support the northern lords. Two months after the rebellion collapsed, on February 25, 1570, he issued a bull, or a written communication from the pope to all Catholics worldwide, on the situation in England. The bull excommunicated Elizabeth, forbidding her membership in the Catholic Church), and called her "the serpent of wickedness." The bull proclaimed that Elizabeth was not rightfully queen, since she had been the child of an illegitimate marriage. The pope encouraged Catholics to rise up against Elizabeth and to help Mary, Queen of Scots, to the throne. The bull arrived in England too late to help the rebel northern lords. Its major effect was to force English Catholics to choose between their loyalty to their queen and their religion. Most chose to ignore the bull.

The uprising and the papal bull made English Protestants view Catholics with suspicion. Even Elizabeth changed her policy. After the bull she treated all Catholic plots as treason rather than religious disagreement. By 1571 a series of acts were passed making it a crime to call the queen a heretic or to use rosary beads, crucifixes, or religious images in one's worship. For the first time, Catholics in England had to be very careful in their religious practices and everyday conversations for fear of being charged with treason.

The Ridolfi Plot

After helping to sponsor the Northern Rising, Roberto Ridolfi, the Florentine banker and agent of the Roman Catholic Church, started another conspiracy against Elizabeth in 1571. His plan called for the Catholic forces of Spain and Rome to invade England and to

Major Catholic Reformation Popes of the Elizabethan Era

1555–59: Pope Paul IV (Giovanni Pietro Caraffa; 1476–1559). An unpopular pope who fought with many European monarchs, especially Philip II of Spain. He was ruthless in stamping out heresy, even accusing some high-ranking Catholic clergy of the crime. When English Queen Mary I strove to reconcile England with the Roman Church in 1554, Paul IV initially refused to settle, demanding to be paid back for the property of the monasteries taken from the church by her father, Henry VIII. On Mary's death he rejected Elizabeth's claim to the crown, claiming she was of illegitimate birth.

1559–65: Pope Pius IV (Giovanni Angelo Medici; 1449–1565). A pope known for successfully bringing about the conclusion of the Council of Trent and for his mildness when treating possible heresy.

1566–72: Pope Pius V (Michele Ghisleri; 1504–1572). Pius V struggled against Protestantism in Germany, France, and the Netherlands. He excommunicated Elizabeth in 1570 and promoted Mary Stuart's right to the throne.

1572–85: Pope Gregory XIII (Ugo Buoncompagni; 1502–1585). Carrying on the fight against Protestant heresy, Gregory XIII was dedicated to creating institutions for the training of Catholic priests to minister to Catholics in Protestant countries like England. After Elizabeth's administrators captured and brutally executed Catholic missionaries, Gregory XIII viewed Elizabeth as a tyrant and an enemy to Catholics. He plotted several times to overthrow her by force. He was detested by Protestants for ordering a celebration in Rome to commemorate the massacre of tens of thousands of Huguenots (French Protestants who followed the teachings of theologian John Calvin) by French Catholics on St. Bartholomew's Day in 1572.

1585–90: Pope Sixtus V (Felice Peretti; 1521–1590). A strong and practical pope who organized and streamlined the church and is today considered one of the great leaders of the Catholic Reformation. He was pope at the beginning of the wars between England and Spain. He renewed the excommunication of Elizabeth in 1588, exonerating from sin anyone who killed the queen. He urged the invasion of England, agreeing to help fund Philip II's Spanish Armada, but only if the mission was successful. He never paid.

immediately promote an uprising of all English Catholics. (According to most historians, Ridolfi grossly overestimated the number of Catholics who would join in the rebellion.) Under this plan the invaders would liberate Mary Stuart. She would quickly marry Howard and together they would seize the English throne. Ridolfi, backed by the pope, tried to enlist the support of Spain's King Philip II (1527–1598), who was initially reluctant to agree to the murder of Elizabeth. Relations between Spain and England were greatly deteriorating, though, and at last he consented to participate, at least in the planning.

Elizabeth had released a repentant Howard from prison after obtaining his promise that he would stay away from Mary Stuart. In February 1571 Mary wrote to him describing Ridolfi's plan. Howard was at first true to his word and refused to go along with the plan, but Mary persisted. By March Howard had agreed to the plot, in which he was to lead the revolt of English Catholics against the queen and her administration. The plan never materialized. The invading Spanish troops were to come from the Netherlands, but the Duke of Alva (1508–1583), the Spanish governor there, distrusted Ridolfi and refused to go along with the plot. In the meantime, England's secretary of state William Cecil (1520–1598) learned of the plans, and Howard was arrested. A search of his residence turned up letters in code from Mary that discussed the plot. Howard confessed his involvement and was found guilty of high treason. Elizabeth always had difficulty authorizing the execution of her close associates. Even after the court found Howard guilty, Elizabeth could not bring herself to consent to his execution. Her worried Privy Council called a special session of Parliament, which demanded that the execution take place. Elizabeth yielded and Howard was beheaded in 1572. Parliament pushed for the execution of Mary, Queen of Scots, as well, but on this issue Elizabeth stood firm. Mary remained in captivity in England for fifteen more years.

English Catholics in exile

When Elizabeth established a Protestant church as the official church of the nation, everyone holding a public or church office or working toward an academic degree was required to swear loyalty to the Act of Supremacy, which declared Elizabeth the supreme governor of all religious matters in England. None of the English Catholic bishops in office when Elizabeth took the throne were willing to swear to the act, and consequently they lost their posts. Under the Act of Uniformity of 1559 all of England's Catholics were fined heavily if they failed attend their local Anglican, or Church of England, service every Sunday. (For more information on the Acts of Supremacy and Uniformity, see Chapter 3.) There was an even bigger fine for attending an illegal Catholic mass. Most Catholics tried to preserve their belief system while outwardly conforming to the Anglican Church. For deeply religious Catholics, however, conforming to the new church went against their most basic beliefs. For them, leaving England was the only choice. Most English Catholics moved to Catholic-friendly countries in Europe.

William Allen and the missionaries to England

One English Catholic exile was William Allen (1532–1594), a prominent educator at Oxford University who was studying for the priesthood when Elizabeth became queen. Allen refused to take the oath of supremacy and in 1561 left England for Louvain, Flanders, where he continued his schooling. (Flanders is a region in present-day northern Belgium.) He returned to England after a year abroad where he secretly ministered to English Catholics. He found Catholics who were eager to practice their faith but, without church or clergy to guide them, they were worshiping in the Protestant churches. After three years Allen, fleeing from the authorities, left England again for the continent. After becoming an ordained priest in Flanders, in 1568 he founded a seminary at Douai (a city in the Spanish Netherlands, now part of present-day France) to train English Catholic exiles as missionaries who would return to England to conduct masses and confessions in secret. Their aim was to preserve the outlawed Catholic faith in any way possible.

By 1574 a small but brave group of Catholic missionaries from Douai and other seminaries had begun to arrive on English shores. The missionaries landed at their own peril; if caught by the English authorities, they were imprisoned and usually tortured under interrogation. Many were brutally executed as traitors. Men who were not of noble birth who were convicted of treason faced the gruesome execution of being hanged, drawn, and quartered. This cruel punishment began with the victim being dragged on a wooden frame to his place of execution, where he was hanged by the neck, but taken down before death. While still alive he was disemboweled—his vital organs were cut out from his body—and the organs were burned before his eyes. Then the body was hacked into four parts, which were usually hung in a public place. Non-noble women convicted of treason were burned at the stake. Nobles of both sexes were generally beheaded.

In 1580, outraged at the deaths of Catholic missionaries, Pope Gregory XIII made a pronouncement that encouraged Elizabeth's murder, saying, as quoted in translation by Alison Weir in *The Life of Elizabeth I,* it would be justified to kill: "that guilty woman who is the cause of so much intriguing to the Catholic faith and loss of so many million souls. There is no doubt that whoever sends her out of the world with the pious intention of doing God service, not only does not sin but gains merit." For the Catholic missionaries who genuinely wished to offer their priestly services and not to overthrow the government, this kind of declaration was disastrous, for it led the English authorities to assume that all Catholic missionaries were spies and conspirators.

Edmund Campion

During the 1560s Edmund Campion (1540–1581) was one of Oxford University's most brilliant scholars. In fact, on a visit to Oxford in 1566, Queen Elizabeth sat in on a debate in which Campion was participating. His intelligence, poise, and knowledge impressed her greatly. At that time Campion was training for the priesthood in the Anglican Church and would almost certainly have become one of the nation's most prominent priests and educators. But Campion had doubts about Protestantism. Like many English citizens at the time, his personal religion had gone through as many upheavals as the country itself. His parents had been Catholic, but Edmund was born in the last years of Henry VIII's reign, after the king had severed ties with the Roman Catholic Church and founded a church based on his own, mostly Catholic, religious notions. When Campion was seven years old, England became a Protestant nation under Edward VI (1537–1553), and Campion and his parents, at least outwardly, converted. When he was thirteen, he, like everyone else, returned to traditional Roman Catholicism under the reign of Mary I. Campion and his parents had again become Protestants in 1559 with Elizabeth's rise to the throne and he had taken the oath of supremacy that was required of him when he took his degree. But his doubts grew and finally led him to convert to Catholicism in 1570. He journeyed to Douai in 1571 to enter the Catholic seminary there, and he was ordained as a Jesuit priest in 1578.

In 1580 the Jesuits began sending missionaries to England; Campion was selected for the first mission. He traveled in the company of another exiled Oxford Jesuit priest, Robert Persons (also spelled Parsons; 1546–1610). Campion knew the dangers that faced him, having heard of the terrible deaths that had befallen some of William Allen's missionaries in England. English authorities had become extremely watchful, with spies looking for Catholic priests throughout the country. Campion arrived in England in disguise. He made his way to London, where he wrote a letter to the Privy Council, which became known as "Campion's Brag." In the letter Campion admitted to being a Jesuit priest who came to England to save souls, but vowed he never had any plans to act against the government.

He confidently added that he was so certain of the truth of the Catholic faith that he would be happy to debate it with any Protestant.

Campion traveled throughout England, constantly trailed by the spies of the government. He hid from authorities in the homes of the wealthy Catholics, particularly those who lived in the northern regions of England. When he arrived in a new district, Catholics gathered from miles around. Campion tirelessly heard their confessions, celebrated the forbidden mass, and conducted marriages or funerals. He was forced to move every few days to avoid capture. Still, Campion and Persons managed to set up a printing press. They published Campion's argument in defense of Catholicism, *Ten Reasons,* and secretly distributed it to the students at Oxford University. Campion's writings quickly spread in secret to England's Catholics.

In the summer of 1581, after numerous close calls, Campion was caught by authorities and placed in the Tower of London, where he was tortured. At his trial the queen's prosecutors claimed, with no proof, that Campion was part of a conspiracy to overthrow Elizabeth and replace her on the throne with Mary Stuart. Campion was quickly convicted of treason, but maintained to the end that he remained a loyal subject to the queen and only differed with her in his religious beliefs.

One day during his imprisonment, without warning, he was brought to a room of the Tower and instructed to debate religious questions with several prominent Protestant theologians who, unlike himself, had been allowed to prepare for the debate. Even in these unfair circumstances, Campion defeated every debater, impressing a large and distinguished audience. He was brought back to debate several other Protestant theologians and excelled each time. Nevertheless, he was brutally executed by being hanged, drawn, and quartered in front of a huge crowd. He was beatified by the Roman Catholic Church in 1886. (Beatification is the first step in the process of becoming a saint, in which a deceased person is officially blessed.)

Campion's mission had been to peacefully save the souls of English citizens, but not all Jesuits were as peaceful as he was. His companion, Parsons, escaped from England and began to seek ways to overthrow Elizabeth's government. He became closely associated with William Allen, who was becoming convinced that Catholicism could not be restored to England by peaceful means. The two become major organizers in conspiracies against Elizabeth involving military and financial support from Spain.

For More Information

BOOKS

Greenblatt, Stephen. *Will in the World: How Shakespeare Became Shakespeare.* New York: Norton, 2004.

Smith, Lacey Baldwin. *The Elizabethan Epic.* London: Panther, 1969.

Watkins, Susan, with photographs by Mark Fiennes. *In Public and in Private: Elizabeth I and Her World.* London: Thames and Hudson, 1998.

Weir, Alison. *The Life of Elizabeth I.* New York: Ballantine Books, 1998.

WEB SITES

"List of Popes." *Catholic Encyclopedia,* Vol. XII. Copyright 2005 by K. Knight. http://www.newadvent.org/cathen/12272b.htm (accessed on July 11, 2006).

Sommerville, J. P. "Elizabethan Catholics." http://history.wisc.edu/sommerville/361/361-18.htm (accessed on July 11, 2006).

———. "The Catholic Reformation" (a list of online primary sources). http://history.wisc.edu/sommerville/361/361-18.htm (accessed on July 11, 2006).

6

Elizabethan Explorers and Colonizers

Euromean exploration of other continents began well before the Elizabethan Era, the period associated with the reign of Queen Elizabeth I (1558–1603) that is often considered to be a golden age in English history. Since Italian explorer Marco Polo (1254–1324) first ventured to Asia in 1266, Europe had enjoyed the exotic merchandise and foods of the faraway lands of China (then called Cathay), India, and the Spice Islands (the Moluccas). For centuries Europeans traveled to these distant markets by land, but in the early 1400s, Middle Eastern natives denied Europeans access to the overland route. Unable to acquire valued goods, Europeans had but one option: to turn to the uncharted oceans. They embarked upon the most significant period of ocean exploration in history.

England was a latecomer to overseas exploration. When Elizabeth (1533–1603) became queen in 1558, the island nation had no available routes for trading in Africa, Asia, or the New World, and it ruled no overseas colonies. Soon, however, independent traders and adventurers of Elizabethan England challenged the great European sea powers and claimed for England a growing, international trade route extending across the known limits of the world.

Portugal and Spain and the Treaty of Tordesillas

Portugal was the first nation to seriously begin sea exploration. Starting around 1420 Portuguese sailors ventured farther and farther down the west coast of Africa; by the end of the century, they had located an eastern route to Asia. In less than fifty years, the sea trade with the ancient lands of Asia lay exclusively in the hands of Portugal. The route was so long it took a year to journey from Portugal to the farthest outpost of its trading empire.

WORDS TO KNOW

ambassador: A high-ranking official who represents his or her own country to the government of another country.

cartography: Mapmaking.

colony: A group of people who settle far from home but remain at least partially under the rule of their homeland.

knight: A man granted a rank of honor by the monarch for his personal merit or service to the country.

latitude: Imaginary lines that run from east to west on the globe measuring the angular distance north or south from the Earth's equator, measured in degrees.

longitude: Imaginary lines drawn on globes or maps that run from north to south, measuring angular distance east or west of the prime meridian, measured in degrees.

monopoly: The exclusive right to trade with a particular market or group of markets.

navigation: The science of setting the course or direction of a ship to get it from one location to another.

privateers: Seafarers who own and operate their own ships independently but are authorized by their government to raid the ships of enemy nations, often capturing the entire ship with all its cargo.

rational: Based on reason rather than on spiritual belief or church authority.

Renaissance: The era beginning around 1350 in Europe, in which scholars turned their attention to classical Greek and Latin learning and shifted to a more rational (based on reason rather than spiritual belief or church authority) approach to philosophy, religion, and science.

In the late fifteenth century Spain was interested in establishing its own overseas trade, but Portugal's control of the only known route to Asia was a major obstacle. A possible solution to the problem was offered in 1492 by Italian explorer Christopher Columbus (1451–1506), who convinced the Spanish queen Isabella (1451–1504) that it was possible to sail west, across the Atlantic, to reach Asia. Isabella agreed to sponsor his expedition, and Columbus sailed off, arriving at the Caribbean islands on October 12, 1492. Columbus believed he had found Asia. He returned to Europe with word of his discovery of the western route to the "Indies," the European name for China, India, and Southeast Asia.

Not long after Columbus arrived in the Caribbean, the Catholic pope ordered the newly discovered lands of the world to be divided between Spain and Portugal, hoping to avoid arguments between Europe's two great Catholic powers. In the Treaty of Tordesillas the pope created a line of demarcation, an imaginary line running north to south on the globe, dividing the world in half. Portugal was given authority to rule all non-Christian lands to the east of the line and Spain was given authority over the lands to the west. No one knew about the geography of the New World yet, and the pope could not have guessed that he had given Spain colonial powers over most of the American continents.

Spanish explorers soon began to journey to various parts of the New World, claiming the land for Spain. The Spanish conquistadors (conquerors) followed, brutally conquering the Aztecs and the Incas, the two most powerful civilizations of the New World, and later destroying the smaller native societies. Over the next three centuries Spain built up its domination of the New World, profiting greatly from its acquisition. Between 1500 and 1650, historians estimate that Spain carried more than 180 tons of gold and 16,000 tons of silver from the New World to Europe. Gold found in the Americas during this period was about ten times more than that discovered in all other countries combined. Spain became one of the wealthiest and most powerful nations in the world.

England's late start

By the time of Elizabeth's reign, Spain had a monopoly, or exclusive right, over all trade with the New World except for Brazil. Portugal monopolized trade with Brazil, as well as over the known sea routes to Asia. France had also become involved in the region, claiming New France, a large area in what is now Canada, in 1534. England, however, had barely begun to explore beyond its own borders.

Elizabeth had no income to support overseas exploration, but she encouraged it for a variety of reasons. First, she felt pressure to develop a trade empire to keep up with her European neighbors. Secondly, by the 1570s Spain's growing power and wealth had begun to threaten England. As part of its mission to unify Europe under the Catholic Church, Spain sought to undermine the rule of the Protestant queen. Though England was too weak to engage in war with Spain in the 1570s, Elizabeth took pleasure in the ability of her seafarers to thwart Spain's mighty powers by raiding its ships and American ports. But what most drew Elizabeth to support English sea adventures was the money she could obtain when her privateers, whom she called "sea dogs," brought home the riches from their raids and gave her the queen's required share.

Privateers were seafarers who owned and operated their own ships but were authorized by the queen to raid the ships of enemy nations. They often seized control of the entire ship and all its cargo, and their violent raids resulted in many deaths. In Elizabethan times there was little

Maps and Navigation

Contrary to common belief, even before Christopher Columbus arrived in the New World in 1492, most educated Europeans accepted that the world was round. Knowledge of the world's geography was far from accurate, however. The maps in use during the Middle Ages (the historical period spanning from c. 500 to c. 1500) were known as *mappa mundi,* or maps of the world. These works of art featured biblical figures or mythical creatures surrounded by distorted outlines of Europe, Africa, and Asia. The edges of the known continents faded into regions believed to be inhabited by monsters and dragons. Although these maps expressed a great deal about medieval culture, they were not very useful for navigation. (Navigation is the science of setting the course or direction of a ship to get it from one location to another.)

During the Renaissance, the era that began around 1350 in Europe, in which scholars turned their attention to classical Greek and Latin learning and shifted to a more rational approach to philosophy, religion, and science, mapmakers in Europe rediscovered the work of the ancient Greek mathematician and geographer Claudius Ptolemy (c. 100–170). Ptolemy had developed the first maps that depicted a round world, and he had also introduced mathematical methods to project the three-dimensional curved lines of the world onto a flat map. Even Ptolemy's maps were too distorted, however, to provide guidance to seafarers. As the sixteenth century began, therefore, most ships sailed only on known courses or within sight of land.

During the sixteenth century residents of the city of Louvain in Flanders (now Belgium) made important advances in the science of cartography, or mapmaking. One of these early pioneers was physician and mathematician Gemma Frisius (1508–1555), who made the first globes of the

Gerard Mercador developed a method for mapping the earth more accurately using longitudinal meridians.
© BETTMANN/CORBIS.

Earth showing the Americas. Globes were the only true models of the world, but they were inadequate navigational tools. Flat maps did not account for the curvature of the Earth. The great challenge looming before mapmakers was mathematical: how to make a two-dimensional model of a three-dimensional sphere.

In 1569 Flemish mathematician and mapmaker Gerard Mercator (1512–1594) found a way to map the Earth accurately enough to be useful to ocean navigators by changing the way the longitudinal meridians were drawn. Longitudinal meridians are the imaginary lines drawn on globes or maps that run from north to south, measuring distances east or west of a selected place called the prime meridian. Mercator made a map of the Earth that depicted the longitudinal meridians running parallel to each other, rather than converging on the two poles, as they do on a globe. Although Mercator's projection distorted the actual sizes of the different regions, its treatment of direction was highly accurate.

England lagged behind other European countries in mapmaking as well as exploration. In fact, as Elizabeth I took the throne in 1558, England had no globes or maps that depicted the New World, and other countries with charts of the seas tended to keep them hidden to avoid competition. The ships in England's navy were frequently forced to sail near shore to navigate. One Englishman, the queen's advisor, mathematician and scientist John Dee (1527–1609), had studied mapmaking with Frisius and Mercator. When the early English

expeditions began to depart for the New World, investors called on Dee to instruct the commanders on the principals of geography, showing them ways to measure their position and set their course.

A variety of navigational tools became available to explorers in the sixteenth century, including the magnetic compass, a navigational instrument for finding directions with an indicator—usually a magnetic needle—that points to the north, and the astrolabe, an instrument that helped pilots calculate latitudinal position (their location in respect to the imaginary east/west lines that cross the surface of the Earth parallel to the equator). Even with the aid of such devices, however, navigation remained a highly inexact science until the seventeenth century.

difference between piracy—high-seas robbery of ships and cargo—and privateering. Elizabeth's involvement in such lawless activities seemed unethical even to some of her own statesmen, including her secretary of state and advisor, William Cecil (1520–1598). To the nations whose ships were raided by the English sea dogs, Elizabeth's failure to stop the lawlessness—and even her apparent encouragement of the raiding—was infuriating. Nonetheless, it was the sea dogs—men like John Hawkins (1532–1595), Francis Drake (c. 1540–1596), and Martin Frobisher (c. 1535–1594)—who established England's powers at sea.

John Hawkins, slave trader

John Hawkins was one of the earliest English seafarers to openly defy the Portuguese and Spanish trade monopolies in Africa and the New World, making overseas trade a legitimate enterprise in England. As a youth Hawkins made a number of voyages to the Spanish-held Canary Islands, where he first learned of the profits to be made from selling African slaves. Soon after Elizabeth became queen, he began to promote the idea of obtaining slaves from Africa and trading them in the New World, where Spanish settlers were desperate for laborers for their sugar mills and mines. Despite the Spanish laws against trading in the Americas, Hawkins was confident that he could trade with the settlers since it was to their benefit.

A group of wealthy merchants formed a company to sponsor Hawkins's slave-trading expedition. Investors bought shares of the company, financing the voyage with their purchases. When Hawkins returned, the shareholders would divide up the expedition's profits in shares equal to those they had purchased. If the expedition failed, however, the sponsors would lose their money. It was to be England's first slave-trading venture, and the first trip by an Englishman into the Caribbean for the purpose of trading.

Hawkins set off for the west coast of Africa with three ships in 1562. When he arrived he kidnapped or traded for an estimated three hundred to eight hundred African men and women. Motivated by the prospects of great financial gain, he treated the African people he captured as if they were non-human cargo. With the Africans on board, Hawkins's fleet left Africa for the Caribbean islands. There he traded the slaves for goods. During his trip he frequently raided Portuguese and Spanish ships, seizing their slaves and goods as well. Even though the Spanish captured two of his ships, Hawkins's first slave trading expedition brought high profits to its investors.

Although many Europeans in Elizabethan times believed that Africans were inferior beings unworthy of normal human consideration, not everyone approved of slavery. In 1563 Queen Elizabeth expressed her own distaste for slave trading, saying, as quoted in *The Queen's Slave Trader: John Hawkyns, Elizabeth I, and the Trafficking in Human Souls* by Nick Hazelwood, "if any African were carried away without their free consent it would be detestable and call down the vengeance of Heaven upon the undertakers." Elizabeth, however, changed her mind when she saw the great profits Hawkins made. She gladly collected a portion of the profits in the name of England.

Hawkins organized a new slave-trading expedition in 1564; this time, high-ranking courtiers and nobles joined with merchants in backing the expedition. Elizabeth loaned Hawkins a ship for the venture, giving him the approval of the English government. When he arrived on the Venezuelan coast, Hawkins found that the Spanish government had forbidden the colonists to trade with him. Having foreseen this possibility, he landed armed parties that, without actually fighting anyone, captured towns long enough to trade with them. Nervous local authorities could later tell Spanish officials that they had been forced to trade with the English, while in truth they desired it. The profits of Hawkins's second voyage far exceeded those of the first.

Back in Spain, King Philip II (1527–1598) was angry. His monopoly over the New World had been granted by the pope; consequently, he considered his authority there to have been granted by God. The Spanish ambassador to England, a high-ranking official who represents his own country to the government of another country, repeatedly complained about Hawkins's violation of the Treaty of Tordesillas. Cecil responded, as quoted by Hazelwood, "that the Pope had no right to partition the world and to give and take kingdoms to whoever (sic) he pleased." With so much money to be made, Elizabeth could not resist encouraging a third expedition.

In 1567 Hawkins sailed for the west coast of Africa once again, this time with a larger fleet, including two ships provided by the queen. His

The fleet of Francis Drake and John Hawkins under attack by the Spanish at San Juan de Ulúa, Mexico. Only two English ships survived the battle. HULTON ARCHIVE/GETTY IMAGES.

young cousin, Francis Drake, was in command of one of the ships. In September 1568, while sailing in the Americas, storms damaged the fleet and it sailed into the port of San Juan de Ulúa, near Veracruz, Mexico. While anchored there, a well-armed Spanish fleet attacked. As Hawkins fought, he saw his men being killed and his ships sunk—all, that is, except Drake's ship, which escaped early in the battle. After heavy losses, Hawkins gathered the scattered survivors on his last remaining ship and escaped. After an agonizing voyage in which many starved or died of thirst, the ship reached England in January 1569. Hawkins resentfully noted, as quoted in Helen Hill Miller's *Captains from Devon: The Great Elizabethan Seafarers Who Won the Oceans for England,* that Drake's ship "forsooke us in our great miserie."

John Hawkins quit slave trading immediately after the disaster at San Juan de Ulúa. His next adventure was to convince King Philip that he would spy on England for him as a double agent. In this way, Hawkins was able to discover plots against Elizabeth. He became a successful merchant and ship builder, and in 1577 Elizabeth made him the lord treasurer of the navy. In this capacity, the former pirate and slave trader became one of the most accomplished statesmen of his time and designed an effective navy for England. (For more information, see Chapter 7).

Francis Drake vows revenge

Francis Drake had disliked Spain and Catholics since his childhood. Humiliated by the attack at San Juan de Ulúa, he bitterly vowed revenge. He would spend the rest of his life ruthlessly and fearlessly fighting Spain.

Drake organized expeditions to the New World in 1569, 1571, and 1572. During the first two voyages, he learned as much as he could about the routes taken by the Spanish fleets hauling gold and silver from the South American mines back to Europe. On his 1572 voyage Drake attacked the port city of Nombre de Dios in Panama, where the Spanish treasure fleet was known to anchor regularly. His crew approached the city banging drums, blaring trumpets, and brandishing torches in order to frighten the residents. The Spanish fled, but not before they had launched a volley of musket fire at Drake and his men. Drake was seriously wounded and soon collapsed. Though the crew had found a hoard of silver, they carried their unconscious captain off to safety, leaving the silver behind.

The small fleet retreated to safer parts of the coast in Panama, where Drake recovered. There the crew became friendly with Cimaroons,

Sir Francis Drake devoted his life to fighting the Spanish.
STOCK MONTAGE/GETTY IMAGES.

former African slaves who had escaped to live with the natives in the forests of the Caribbean islands and South America. The Cimaroons hated the Spanish and were glad to help Drake's fleet harass them. With their advice Drake planned the successful ambush of a mule train near Nombre de Dios. (A mule train is a group of travelers carrying goods on mules.) The mule train was carrying so much gold and silver, however, Drake and his crew had difficulty transporting it all to the fleet. They carried as much gold as they could to the shore, where they built a raft to float it to their awaiting ships. The enormous bounty Drake brought back to England made him an instant national hero and a very wealthy man. He also became the hated enemy of King Philip.

Drake circumnavigates the globe

During his stay in Panama, the Cimaroons had taken Drake to a point on the isthmus (the narrow strip of land in Panama connecting Central and South America) from which he was able to view the Pacific Ocean. He dreamed of one day sailing up the west coast of South America. He had his chance in 1577. With all his successes Drake had become a favorite of Elizabeth. Cecil worried about Drake's rash behavior, but the queen and some of her other councilors viewed the seemingly unstoppable sea dog as a one-man weapon against the arrogant Spanish. It did not hurt that Elizabeth prospered in her share of the wealth from his extremely successful raids on Spain's ships. With the backing of several high-ranking noblemen in Elizabeth's closest circle, Drake began to secretly prepare to explore the Pacific Coast of the New World. The plans for the expedition were so secret that not even the crew that was to accompany him knew its mission. Elizabeth herself invested in Drake's expedition, but she kept its destination secret from Cecil, knowing he did not approve of Drake's piracy on the seas.

On December 13, 1577, Drake set out in his ship, the *Golden Hind,* with a fleet of five large and well-armed ships. The expedition sailed from Plymouth, England, to the Cape Verde Islands, a group of Portuguese-controlled islands off the northwest coast of Africa. Drake then headed west, toward Brazil, and south down the east coast of South America. The ships anchored on June 18, 1578, at San Julián, in present-day southern Argentina, at the entrance to the Strait of Magellan. (The Strait of Magellan is a body of water at the southern end of South America that connects the Atlantic and Pacific Oceans.)

Storms had taken their toll on the fleet, and after wintering at San Julián, only three ships were able to continue on the seventeen-day passage through the Strait of Magellan. More heavy storms in the Strait battered the ships, sinking one and causing the *Golden Hind* to lose sight of the other. The *Golden Hind* was blown far south of its course. There was a widely held belief at the time that a huge continent called Terra Australis lay south of South America. The accidental side trip confirmed what Drake had suspected—the southern border of the Strait was in fact formed by a large group of islands, not a continent. This was an important contribution to geographical knowledge of the day.

Traveling up the Pacific Coast of South America alone, the *Golden Hind* began its raids on the unprepared Spanish ships and ports. Because the Pacific Coast had been solely in their control for many decades, the Spanish had never built up proper systems of defense. Drake began by capturing a large trading ship in the port of Valparaíso, in Chile, and then raided the town itself. He then proceeded up the coast, capturing trading vessels and port towns. On March 1, 1579, the *Golden Hind* overpowered a huge Spanish ship brimming with gold, silver, and jewels and stole its treasure.

Drake was ready to return to England but, having left many angry Spaniards in his wake, he did not want to sail back the way he had come. At that time it was generally believed that a strait called the Northwest Passage ran through North America. Drake headed as far north as Vancouver, British Columbia, in present-day Canada, searching unsuccessfully for the strait. When it did not appear, he sailed south again to San Francisco Bay, where he spent a month restocking food and supplies and repairing the ship. The local Coast Miwok Indians—who had seen the *Golden Hind* arrive from the west, the land of dead ancestors—assumed Drake and his men must be gods. Drake misunderstood the Miwoks' respect as a surrender of their land to the English queen. He took possession of the region, calling it *New Albion.* (Albion is a poetic name for England.)

Now convinced that there was no strait through North America, Drake realized he would have to cross the Pacific to get home. In July 1579 the *Golden Hind* began a two-month westward voyage through the Philippines, the Moluccas (also known as the Spice Islands), Timor and Java, around the Cape of Good Hope at the southernmost point of the African continent, and up the Atlantic coast of Africa. Drake's ship arrived back in England in 1580, nearly three years after the voyage began.

Drake's expedition was only the second voyage ever to have circumnavigated, or gone all the way around, the globe. England's attention, though, was focused on the magnificent treasures Drake had brought back with him. His bounty was valued at £326,580. For each pound invested in the expedition, investors received £47. Elizabeth, though greatly enriched by her investment, initially kept silent about the voyage so as not to disrupt the peace negotiations she was conducting with Spain.

Six months after the return of the *Golden Hind,* though, the queen boarded Drake's ship to celebrate his feat with him. She wore a jeweled crown and a diamond cross Drake had given her. After dinner aboard the ship, the queen knighted Drake. (A knight is a man granted a rank of honor by the monarch for his personal merit or service to the country.) From his beginnings as a poor lad in Devon, Drake had risen to become a wealthy and famous man.

Martin Frobisher and the Northwest Passage

Since the Spanish controlled the western route to Asia around the southern tip of the Americas and the Portuguese controlled the eastern routes around Africa, the English, Dutch, and French had long sought alternative routes to Asia. Many believed that a Northwest Passage through North America existed that would allow them to sail on to China. A few English explorers had ventured to the cold shores of Greenland and present-day Canada seeking the passage before Elizabeth's time, but during her reign the search began in earnest.

In 1566 Sir Humphrey Gilbert (1539–1583), a nobleman, member of Parliament, and explorer who studied the geography of ancient philosophers, wrote *A Discourse of a Discovery for a New Passage to Cataia (China)*, in which he attempted to persuade Elizabeth to support an expedition seeking a Northwest Passage to China. She turned him down. Gilbert's lobbying eventually convinced Elizabeth, but she chose to grant a license instead to Martin Frobisher to explore the northern seas around North America in 1575.

Frobisher had a colorful past. As a child, he had been on trading voyages to West Africa, and he had been held hostage by an African chief. After serving in the English army, he became a privateer. During the 1560s Frobisher was repeatedly arrested for piracy, and most of his countrymen looked down on him as a common criminal.

During his years of privateering, Frobisher became fascinated with the idea of the Northwest Passage, and in 1575 he persuaded a group of investors to finance a search for it. Frobisher left England in 1576 in command of two small ships. Sailing northwest from England, they arrived on the coast of Greenland. There, the two ships were separated in a storm, and one returned to England. Frobisher continued to sail westward. Eventually the great inlet on Baffin Island, later named Frobisher Bay, came into his view. Though supplies were running low and the temperatures were so cold that a thick shield of ice coated the

Explorer Martin Frobisher attempted to discover the Northwest Passage. PUBLIC DOMAIN.

entire ship, he sailed on, convinced he had found the passageway to Asia. After exploring and encountering the native population, the Inuits, the ship returned to England.

Frobisher's crew had found a black rock with shiny elements in it on an island in Frobisher Bay, and they brought a sample home with them. Some goldsmiths believed the rock contained deposits of real gold. This discovery stimulated interest in Frobisher's quest, and he was able to finance another trip. Even Elizabeth invested in the expedition and supplied him with a ship. In May 1577 Frobisher set off with three ships. When he reached Frobisher Bay his crew loaded about two hundred tons of black rock onto his ships and brought it back to England. Although some of Frobisher's partners realized that the rock he had brought back was worthless, enough interest remained to send out another, even larger expedition in 1578.

The new expedition carried settlers and supplies to build an English colony in the newly discovered land. (A colony is a group of people who settle far from home but remain at least partially under the rule of their homeland.) The settlers would mine the rock, if it proved to be valuable. The fleet arrived again in Frobisher Bay, where Frobisher built a stone house that was found there almost three hundred years later. Frobisher's expedition returned to England without much to show for its efforts. Metal workers tried to refine the black rocks into gold but failed. The investors in the expedition had lost their money, and Frobisher gave up his dream of finding the Northwest Passage.

Humphrey Gilbert's colony

In the 1570s Humphrey Gilbert began to promote the establishment of an English colony on the Atlantic Coast of North America. He was not alone in this idea. John Dee also urged colonization in 1577 in his four-volume work *General and Rare Memorials Pertaining to the Perfect Art of Navigation.* It was Dee who coined the term "English Empire" that would become so important in the years ahead.

In 1578 Elizabeth granted Gilbert a charter to settle any lands in the New World that were not already ruled by a Christian prince. With the assistance of his half brother, Walter Raleigh (1522–1618), Gilbert set out on his first expedition. He was attacked by Spaniards and forced to return to England. Gilbert lost his money and spent the next few years raising funds for a new expedition. Gilbert's second expedition of five ships left England in 1583, reaching the northern coast of Newfoundland at the end of July and then sailing into the harbor at St. John's, now the capital and largest city in Newfoundland. Gilbert claimed the site for the queen, and he and the other colonists stayed there for two weeks. Gilbert intended to return the following year. Unfortunately, on the voyage back to England, Gilbert's ship sank in a storm. Everyone on board, including Gilbert, drowned.

Explorer Humphrey Gilbert drowned when his ship sank in a storm. Gilbert was returning from an expedition to Newfoundland. HULTON ARCHIVE/GETTY IMAGES.

Virginia

After Gilbert's death Walter Raleigh felt it was his duty to carry out his brother's mission of establishing a colony in the New World. Before choosing a site, Raleigh sent a small survey party to explore an area in present-day North Carolina. They returned with a favorable report, finding the site inviting and fertile, with a climate far milder than that of Newfoundland. Raleigh claimed the entire region stretching along the

Atlantic Coast between present-day North Carolina and Maine for England. He named the new land Virginia after Elizabeth, the Virgin Queen.

Raleigh needed funding to establish a colony. He was one of Elizabeth's favorites and she had made him a knight, but she did not offer him any money for the expedition. Raleigh turned for help to one of the most influential writers of his time, Richard Hakluyt (pronounced HAK-loot; c. 1552–1616). Hakluyt was fascinated with geography and exploration. In 1580 he had written his *Discourse on the Strait of Magellan*, calling for exploration of the Northwest Passage, and in 1582 he compiled *Diverse Voyages to America*, a collection of explorers' documents. His writing raised the public interest in exploring the New World. Raleigh persuaded Hakluyt to write a memorial to the queen, hoping it would persuade her to lend financial support to his new venture. Hakluyt drafted the memorial, known as *A Discourse on Western Planting* ("planting" refers to establishing colonies), which put forth nearly every argument to support English colonization that would be advanced over the next two centuries. Elizabeth offered her encouragement, but no money.

The first Roanoke Island colony

In 1585, finally having raised enough money, Raleigh dispatched an expedition of about one hundred settlers to establish a colony in Virginia. Raleigh had hoped to command the expedition himself, but Elizabeth, fearful of losing her favorite, would not allow him to go. The colonists made a slow crossing and arrived at Roanoke Island, in present-day North Carolina, too late to plant crops. The ship's captain immediately returned to England for more supplies. The colonists built a fort and a few dwellings, but most of them spent their time in an unsuccessful search for gold rather than working the land or finding food sources. Among the colonists were a young Oxford scholar, Thomas Harriot (1560–1621), and an artist, John White (died c. 1593). They had been sent to record the plants and people of the region and map out the territory. They later used their experience to provide England with its first accurate descriptions and illustrations of the New World.

As the colonists' supply shortages grew worse, resources had to be obtained from the native inhabitants of the land, the Roanokes, Croatoans, and Secotans. The natives initially helped the newcomers, but as the English demanded more food and goods, the native people became increasingly hostile. By the summer of 1586 the colonists were out of supplies and ready to leave. Francis Drake happened to be on a raiding expedition in the Caribbean that summer. After ransacking the Spanish colony at St. Augustine, Florida, he sailed up the coast to Roanoke Island. He offered to take the colonists home and they gladly accepted. They had lasted about ten months in the colony.

The "lost colony" at Roanoke

In 1587 Raleigh made a second attempt to establish a permanent colony in Virginia. He gathered eighty-four men, seventeen women, and nine children to settle there under the authority of John White, whom he named deputy governor. The settlers once again chose Roanoke Island for their colony. Another supply shortage forced a reluctant White to leave his own family behind and return to England. Only nine days before he left, his daughter had given birth to Virginia Dare, the first English child to be born on American soil. Back in England, White loaded two boats with supplies, but as he prepared to return to Virginia, England and Spain went to war in the famous 1588 battle of the Spanish Armada. (For more information on the Spanish Armada, see Chapter 7). White could not sail for America until 1590. When he arrived at Roanoke, the colony had disappeared. The only sign he found was the word "CROATOAN" carved on a tree. No one knows what happened to the lost colony, but most scholars agree that the colonists probably headed inland to live with the Croatoans.

Raleigh gave up on colonizing, but many lessons had been learned from his failed efforts. It was clear that no single individual could finance a settlement. It was also clear that the Spanish experience of discovering vast wealth in gold and silver mines in South America would not be repeated. In North America different kinds of economic opportunities existed, such as farming, logging, and fishing, which would require planning and labor. Colonists needed to prepare themselves for hard work and harsh conditions. Raleigh's endeavors captured English interest in building an overseas empire. Within decades, others would follow in his footsteps and, armed with better information, they would succeed in building England's first permanent colonies.

In 1589 Richard Hakluyt published his first edition of *Principle (sic) Navigations, Voyages, and Discoveries of the English Nation.* It championed the idea of turning to farming to establish strong, profitable, and permanent colonies. Hakluyt argued that permanent colonies would keep Spain out of North America, secure a new source of badly needed raw materials for England's industries, and create a new market for English exports. He also saw the New World as the ideal place to send England's poor, unemployed, and criminal elements. This widely read book was very persuasive in promoting colonization of North America.

For More Information

BOOKS

Brimacombe, Peter. *All the Queen's Men: The World of Elizabeth I.* New York: St. Martin's Press, 2000.

Hazelwood, Nick. *The Queen's Slave Trader: John Hawkyns, Elizabeth I, and the Trafficking in Human Souls.* New York: William Morrow, 2004.

Miller, Helen Hill. *Captains from Devon: The Great Elizabethan Seafarers Who Won the Oceans for England.* Chapel Hill, NC: Algonquin Books, 1985.

Woolley, Benjamin. *The Queen's Conjurer: The Science and Magic of Dr. John Dee, Adviser to Queen Elizabeth I.* New York: Henry Holt and Company, 2001.

PERIODICALS

Crane, Nicholas. "Changing Our World View." *Geographer,* April 2003, p. 33.

Marsh, Katherine. "Truth in Mapping: Gerard Mercator." *U.S. News and World Report,* February 23, 2004, p. 65.

WEB SITES

"Elizabeth's Pirates." http://www.channel4.com/history/microsites/H/history/pirates/pirates1.html (accessed on July 11, 2006).

Kraus, Hans P. "The Famous Voyage: The Circumnavigation of the World 1577–1580," *Sir Francis Drake: A Pictorial Biography.* Published in Amsterdam by N. Israel, 1970. Copyright © 1970 by H. P. Kraus. Library of Congress: Rare Books and Special Collections Reading Room. http://www.loc.gov/rr/rarebook/catalog/drake/drake-home.html (accessed on July 11, 2006).

7

The War with Spain

During the 1560s and 1570s Queen Elizabeth I (1533–1603; reigned 1558–1603) kept England out of all major wars. She consistently hesitated to act on advice she received from her Privy Council, the board of advisors that administered her government. This frustrated the Council enormously, for they often felt that England should rush into military action. In hindsight, however, her indecision may have served England well. The two decades of peace allowed England to build its economic and military power, bringing stability and prosperity to the land.

With her religious settlement of 1559, Elizabeth had aimed to secure internal peace by unifying England under one church. (For more information on Elizabeth's religious settlement, see Chapter 3.) She allowed those who had been raised in the Catholic Church to believe what they liked as long as they conformed outwardly to the new Anglican Church. She knew that within a generation or two, those who had been raised in the Catholic religion would die off and younger generations would have no memory of the traditional church. Her efforts were highly successful. By the 1570s the majority of English Catholics were loyal to the queen; many satisfied themselves with practicing forbidden traditions (such as the Catholic mass and confession) only in private. The younger generations would never fully experience the tradition that had been lost.

The peaceful, but complete, end of Catholicism in England that Elizabeth envisioned was intolerable to many Catholics abroad. The Roman Catholic Church gathered its forces against the English queen, viewing her as the one great obstacle in the way of bringing England back to its traditional religion. Far more dangerous to Elizabeth was her former brother-in-law, the Spanish king Philip II (1527–1598), who had gradually come to view the restoration of Catholicism to England as his divine mission. By the early 1580s Spain had become the greatest threat to England's security.

WORDS TO KNOW

armada: The Spanish word for a fleet of ships.

cardinal: A top official in the Roman Catholic Church, ranking just below the pope.

Counter Reformation: Also called the Catholic Reformation; the period beginning in the 1520s when the Catholic Church, partially in response to the rise of Protestantism, tried to reunify Europe under Catholicism and to spread Roman Catholic Christianity to the New World, Asia, and Africa.

heresy: A religious opinion that conflicts with the church's doctrines.

Holy Roman Empire: A loose confederation of states and territories, including the German states and most of central Europe, that existed from 962 to 1806 and was considered the supreme political body of the Christian people.

privateers: Seafarers who own and operate their own ships independently but are authorized by their government to raid the ships of enemy nations, often capturing the entire ship with all its cargo.

Privy Council: The board of advisors that carried out the administrative function of the government in matters of economy, defense, foreign policy, and law and order, and its members served as the king's or queen's chief advisors.

Reformation: A sixteenth-century religious movement that aimed to reform the Roman Catholic Church and resulted in the establishment of Protestant churches.

Philip II

Spain became the dominant power in Europe in 1492; its formerly independent provinces united in the same year that explorer Christopher Columbus (1451–1506) made his historic voyage to the New World. This year also marked the beginning of Spain's colonial empire. Spain's army quickly earned fame, winning every land battle in which it fought for more than a century. In 1516 Charles V (1500–1558) became the king of Spain. Charles was also the Holy Roman Emperor, the leader of a loose confederation of states and territories that included the German states and most of central Europe. His inheritance of Spain and other regions gave him control of a major portion of Europe. Charles decided to divide up his empire in 1554, giving Spain and the Netherlands to his son, Philip. At that time Spain included all of present-day Spain, plus the southern part of present-day Italy—Naples, Sardinia, and Sicily—and Spain's overseas colonies—most of South and Central America and parts of Africa. The Netherlands, also called the Lowlands, at the time included present-day Belgium, Luxembourg, the

Map of the European regions under Spain's control during the reign of Philip II. MAP BY XNR PRODUCTIONS. THE GALE GROUP.

present-day Netherlands, and parts of France and Germany. Philip had become the ruler of a vast and powerful empire.

Philip was a very restrained, hard-working king. He was a quiet man, preferring solitude and work to court and society. The Spanish king trusted no one and did not allow others to help him with the duties of running a large kingdom. He reviewed every government document, analyzed the accounts, and deliberated painfully over every decision, whether large or small. His military forces were the most powerful in Europe, but they were made less effective by the fact that they were frequently forced to wait for word from the king himself before taking action.

Philip was a devout Catholic. As early as 1573 he had signed a treaty with Pope Gregory XIII (1502–1585), agreeing to invade England and exterminate Protestant heresy there. But Philip distrusted the pope, and he chose to control the Spanish Catholic church himself. The pope feared

King Philip II of Spain considered it his divine mission to restore Catholicism to England. PUBLIC DOMAIN.

Philip. The power of the church in Rome would be greatly reduced if Philip became the supreme ruler in Europe. The extreme distrust between the pope and the Spanish king hindered the mission to restore Catholicism to England.

Hostilities grew very slowly between Spain and England. Philip initially respected Elizabeth. He had protected her when his wife, Queen Mary I (1516–1558), had been determined to execute Elizabeth as a traitor. He had even proposed marriage to Elizabeth after Mary died. Though his motives for the proposal were certainly political, in the first two decades of Elizabeth's reign, Philip seemed willing to accept her as queen (though always under careful watch), perhaps believing that she would soon come to her senses and return to the Catholic religion. Like Elizabeth, Philip was hesitant to go to war. Despite the great wealth brought into Spain from the gold and silver mines in the New World, the Spanish economy was weak, particularly because of conflicts in the Netherlands.

It was around 1580 that Philip started planning the "Enterprise of England," a plan to invade and conquer the island, starting with building a great fleet of war ships known as the Armada (the Spanish word for "fleet"). He had many reasons to choose war. For Philip the primary reason was religious: he believed it was his obligation to God to eliminate Protestant heresy from Europe. But it was also an attempt at territorial conquest. With England under Spanish rule, Philip would have a strategic foothold over a large area of western Europe, expanding his vast empire as well as his religion. War was also a reaction to what Philip considered bad behavior on Elizabeth's part: her aid to rebels against him in the Netherlands, English raids of Spanish ships (see Chapter 6), and finally the execution of Mary Stuart, Queen of Scots (1542–1587), who was considered by many Catholics to be the rightful queen of England.

Rebellion in the Netherlands

The Spanish economy had come to depend on the tax revenue raised in the Netherlands, which had become an extremely prosperous center of international trade. Philip, who never set foot in the Netherlands after 1559, had little understanding of the Dutch. Trying to organize the small states in his own way, he disregarded the traditional authority of the local governments. Moreover, when Protestantism was embraced in the northern areas of the Netherlands (located in the present-day Netherlands) in the 1560s, Philip took strong measures to stamp it out completely.

Resistance to his harsh rule and taxation increased until, in 1566, the large cities of the Netherlands rose up in rebellion. Philip sent in Spanish troops to subdue the rebels, and a war for national independence began that would continue throughout Philip's reign. In 1579 the primarily Protestant rebels in the north declared themselves independent. The southern part (the area roughly comprising present-day Belgium) was mainly Catholic and was persuaded for a time to remain under Spanish control. Philip's armies renewed their efforts in the northern territories.

Some of Philip's advisors were convinced that Protestant England and its queen were supporting the rebels in the Netherlands. They called for the invasion, believing they could subdue the Netherlands if England was under Spanish control. Others advised the king that it would be folly to try to invade England without already having a firm base in the Netherlands.

Elizabeth's foreign policy

For many years England's foreign policy had been dependent on the relations between the two larger European powers of France and Spain. Traditionally Spain and France had been enemies. England had been friendly with Spain and hostile to France. By the 1570s, however, Spain and France had negotiated a fragile peace. France had been torn apart by religious wars between the Huguenots (French Calvinists, or Protestants) and the Catholic French government, making Spain by far the most powerful empire. If Philip cemented his rule over the Netherlands, England would face a block of Catholic, and possibly hostile, nations of Europe directly across the English Channel. Elizabeth intended to prevent such consolidation of power.

Elizabeth hoped to join forces, at least temporarily, with the French. France was ruled by Catherine de Médici (1519–1589), the mother of France's young King Charles. De Médici was a notorious schemer who provoked France's religious conflict. By pitting the Huguenots against the Catholic dukes of France, she hoped to increase the power of her sons. Her scheming caused nine bloody religious wars and hundreds of thousands of deaths, including the massacre of tens of thousands of Huguenots on St. Batholemew's Day in 1572. (For more information on the St. Bartholemew's Day Massacre, See Chapter 4.) Many members of Elizabeth's Privy Council, horrified to see fellow Protestants in danger, urged the queen to aid the Huguenots. Elizabeth, though disgusted with the slaughter, preferred to maintain diplomatic relations with France as a defense against Spanish control of western Europe.

Marriage between monarchs had long been the favored means of establishing alliances among nations, and Elizabeth preferred courtship to war. De Médici eagerly offered each of her three sons to marry the English queen. The first two were quickly dismissed, but when de Médici sent her third son, François, Duke of Alençon (1555–1584), to court Elizabeth in 1579, the forty-five-year-old queen unexpectedly responded enthusiastically, and even showed signs of falling in love with her suitor. She called Alençon her "little frog" (he had been badly scarred by small-pox as a child), wrote him poems, kissed him in public, and gave him her ring. Many historians believe that Elizabeth only made a show of love and interest in marriage in the interest of a political alliance with France, but others argue that she had developed genuine feelings for him. Regardless of her intentions, opposition in England to this marriage to the detested French royalty was very high; in fact, it was clear that an uprising might result if the queen were to marry her suitor. Elizabeth gave up the match.

In 1585 Spanish forces captured the Dutch commercial capital of Antwerp (in modern-day Belgium). With Spanish troops less than one hundred miles from London, Elizabeth was finally persuaded by her Privy Council to send a small army to aid the Dutch revolt. Robert Dudley (Earl of Leicester; 1532–1588), her longtime favorite, took command of a force of seven thousand soldiers and set off to help the rebels. But the English forces did little to help the Dutch rebels, and in 1587 Elizabeth called Dudley back to London. Nevertheless, her commitment of troops was a key factor in convincing Philip to wage war on England.

Francis Drake, the Master Thief of the Unknown World

On the open seas, English privateers gave Philip further reason for war. (Privateers are seafarers who own and operate their own ships independently but are authorized by their government to raid the ships of enemy nations, often capturing the entire ship with all its cargo.) In 1585, enraged by English raids on his ships, Philip made a plan to strike back. His ministers let it be known that Spain needed to purchase wheat to feed its troops. English merchants responded, sending ships filled with wheat to sell to Spanish ports. But Spanish soldiers seized the English ships, cargo and all. Elizabeth responded in kind by issuing "letters of marque" to any merchant or ship owner who had lost a ship or goods to the Spanish. These letters authorized the holder to seize any

Spanish ships they encountered on the seas to compensate for the amount they had lost. Many English ship owners were experienced pirates (robbers on the high seas, who seized ships and their cargo). Among the English raiders, no one inspired as much fear and awe among Spaniards as Francis Drake (c. 1540–1596), whom they called the Master Thief of the Unknown World.

Drake was the most famous and successful English privateer. In his youth Drake had developed a life-long hatred for the Spanish, and began raiding Spanish ships in the 1560s. He learned the routes of the ships transporting gold and silver from the New World and raided Spanish ports in the Americas, all with great success. Elizabeth pretended to disapprove because she was engaged in peacekeeping negotiations with Spain, but she privately encouraged Drake in his raids and happily accepted a significant portion of the vast riches he seized from the Spanish. (For more information on Drake and other English privateers, see Chapter 6.)

In 1585, with hostilities between England and Spain high, Drake outfitted a twenty-three-ship fleet that included two of the queen's own vessels and set off to attack Spanish ports. He first attacked the port of Vigo in Galicia (a territory in northwest Spain). He then sailed to Santo Domingo (the capital of Spain's American empire and the present-day capital of the Dominican Republic) and Cartagena (a large and wealthy port on the north coast of Colombia that was the center of the silver trade), raiding both ports. On his way back to England, Drake also attacked the Spanish settlement at St. Augustine, Florida. The expedition greatly damaged the Spanish fleet.

In 1587 Drake led a naval attack on the Spanish port of Cadiz, where his small fleet surprised a large number of Spanish warships. Drake burned and sank a number of ships and slipped away before the Spanish could recover. Despite his success Drake could see that the Spanish Armada was a formidable enemy and sent word warning the English to prepare themselves. Elizabeth, though, was trying to negotiate with Philip in the hope of preventing war. To avoid further hostility, she prevented the frustrated Drake from resuming his raids.

But Philip's intentions toward England were no longer peaceful. He was infuriated that Elizabeth had not stopped the lawless behavior of English privateers. Along with damaging Philip's fleet and stealing his gold and silver, Drake and the other privateers had badly disrupted the Spanish economy. Merchants and traders, fearing privateer raids, chose

Francis Drake led a successful attack on the Spanish port of Cadiz in 1587. HULTON ARCHIVE/GETTY IMAGES.

not to transport goods from the New World that were essential to Spain and the support of Philip's troops. Although Philip continued to negotiate with Elizabeth, he was only stalling for time as he built up his Armada and prepared to invade England.

Plots surrounding the Queen of Scots

The many political plots surrounding Mary Stuart, Queen of Scots, also influenced Philip's decision to go to war against England. After the plots of the early 1570s to replace Elizabeth on the English throne, Mary Stuart had lived for well over a decade as a prisoner in England. (For more information, see Chapter 5.) She continued to smuggle letters to the pope, her relatives in France, and Philip, hoping to persuade them to invade England and place her on its throne. Few of her contacts were interested in helping her. Initially Philip did not support Mary Stuart. He was disgusted by her immoral behavior and distrusted her strong connection to the French. Philip worried that the French would gain influence and power in England if Mary took the throne. But by the early 1580s tension between England and Spain convinced him that Elizabeth might be worse than her Scottish cousin.

In 1582 Mary convinced Spain's ambassador in England that, given a bit of help from abroad, English Catholics would rise up in great numbers to rebel against Elizabeth. The ambassador conspired with a young English Catholic nobleman, Francis Throckmorton (1554–1584) in a plot to overthrow Elizabeth and liberate Mary. Elizabeth's councilors learned of the plan and arrested Throckmorton, who, under torture, told the details of the plot. He was executed and the Spanish ambassador was expelled from the country. Plots involving Mary continued to surface, though, and the Privy Council and English Parliament called once again for the execution of Mary Stuart. Elizabeth hesitated to kill a sovereign. She did not believe that any court had the authority to pass judgment on a sovereign queen.

Francis Walsingham, spymaster

In 1573 Elizabeth had promoted her secretary of state, William Cecil (Lord Burghley; 1520–1598), to become the lord high treasurer. She replaced him as secretary with Francis Walsingham (1532–1590), a Puritan, a member of a group of radical Protestants who followed the teachings of Swiss theologian John Calvin, and former ambassador to France. Over the years Walsingham had constructed an intricate network of spies throughout Europe to keep track of the Catholic conspiracies against Elizabeth and other Protestants. As Elizabeth's chief councilor in charge of security, he was determined to eliminate the threat posed by Mary Stuart.

In 1585 Walsingham developed a plan. He convinced Gilbert Gifford, a Catholic spy and one of Mary's trusted messengers, to become a double agent working for Elizabeth. Gifford established a secret system of communication for Mary in which her letters, written in code, could be smuggled out of her residence concealed in the boards of beer kegs. Correspondence from abroad could be smuggled to her in the same way. What Mary did not know was that Walsingham had arranged to see every piece of correspondence before it was delivered. He even had a special school where the letters were sent for decoding. In this way he

Queen Elizabeth I and her secretary of state, Sir Francis Walsingham, discuss the conspiracy of Anthony Babington and Mary Stuart, who planned to murder Elizabeth. HULTON ARCHIVE/ GETTY IMAGES.

hoped to collect enough evidence to convict Mary of treason. It was not long before Walsingham's plan succeeded.

A Jesuit priest named John Ballard arrived in England in 1586 to initiate an uprising of English Catholics supported by an invasion of the Spanish military. He contacted Anthony Babington (1561–1586), a young nobleman who had once served as a page, or attendant, to Mary Stuart. Like most men who came into contact with the beautiful and persuasive queen of Scots, Babington was devoted to her and he was eager to take part in a plot against the Protestant government. In July 1586 Babington wrote to Mary, communicating the details of his plan to kill

Elizabeth with the help of six of his friends so that Mary could take the throne. In a long letter intercepted by Walsingham, Mary agreed to the Babington plot, including the murder of Elizabeth. Babington and his friends were arrested and confessed to the plot, acknowledging Mary's involvement in it. Her treason was at last a proven fact.

The execution of Mary Stuart

England was in an uproar; nearly everyone demanded Mary's execution. Elizabeth still did not want to be held responsible for her cousin's death, particularly because Mary's son, James VI of Scotland (1566–1625), was one of her few allies. She asked the noblemen who guarded Mary to murder her in her sleep, but no one was willing to risk it. After a great deal of hesitation, Elizabeth finally signed the death warrant. However, instead of ordering it delivered to the place of execution, she dramatically

Mary Stuart receiving her death warrant. HULTON ARCHIVE/GETTY IMAGES.

threw it on the floor. Her councilors picked it up and, without further authorization, sent it to the prison where the queen of Scots was held. Afterwards Elizabeth could pretend she had not been responsible for the execution.

On February 8, 1587, Mary Stuart was beheaded in front of her weeping ladies-in-waiting and three hundred spectators. Dressed in a blood-red bodice and petticoat as a sign that she was a martyr (someone who accepts punishment or death rather than deny their religious convictions) of the Catholic Church, Mary faced her death with courage and composure, calmly committing herself to God before the axe fell. Protestants in England celebrated the death of Mary Stuart, but Catholic Europe mourned. The pope called for war against England and urged Philip to invade. He also gave permission to Philip to name a new heir to the English throne to replace Mary Stuart. Philip named his own daughter as the rightful queen of England and began his final plans for invasion.

England prepares for war

As late as the summer of 1587 Elizabeth was still trying to negotiate peace with Spain. Her commissioners discussed terms with the commander of the Spanish forces in the Netherlands, Alessandro Farnese, Duke of Parma and Piacenza (1545–1592). In the spring of 1588 a dismayed Elizabeth learned that Philip had designated his daughter as the rightful queen of England. She began preparations for a Spanish attack.

Every soldier and statesman in England understood that if Spanish troops were able to successfully invade English shores, England could not win a land battle. There were only a few hundred professional soldiers scattered throughout the whole nation. In an invasion, local militias, or groups of volunteers, would be responsible for defending most of the country. Hastily formed and mostly unarmed and untrained, these militias could not win against the superior armies of Spain. In fact it would have been nearly impossible to protect every port in England from invasion, and no one knew where Philip intended to attack.

England had a small but outstanding navy, thanks largely to Elizabeth's father, Henry VIII (1491–1547). At his death the English navy included fifty-three warships. They were expensive to maintain, though, and by the time of Mary I's reign, the navy had diminished to thirty ships. Philip, as Mary's husband, had argued strongly in favor of building up England's navy, considering it the country's best means of defense. He could not have foreseen that, thirty years later, Spain would be battling the very ships he had advocated.

Since becoming queen Elizabeth had devoted her resources to maintaining and building up the English navy. According to most historians she made a brilliant choice in her 1578 appointment of the former slave-trader and privateer John Hawkins (1532–1595) as treasurer of the navy. (For more information on Hawkins's slave trade, see Chapter 6.) Hawkins developed a new kind of warship that was much lighter, faster, and easier to operate than earlier ships. He trained a small, elite group of highly skilled and motivated sailors, giving them better working conditions and higher wages in return for top performance. Hawkins, more than anyone else, was responsible for making the English fleet the most modern navy in the world. Elizabeth's navy numbered about thirty-four ships in 1588, and thirty private vessels armed for battle also volunteered to fight the Spanish Armada.

Elizabeth chose talented commanders for the English fleet. The top command was given to her cousin, Admiral Lord (Charles) Howard of Effingham (1536–1624). Second in command officers included Francis Drake, John Hawkins, and explorer and privateer Martin Frobisher (c. 1535–1594), among others. Lord Howard had the least amount of sea experience, but he was an outstanding commander who knew how to utilize the skills and experience of his captains.

English strategy in a naval battle was simple. They knew they could not compete in hand-to-hand combat with the skilled Spaniards, who would try to board their ships. To avoid being boarded, the English fleet prepared to use long-range cannons to fire at the Spanish ships from a safe distance. Elizabeth gave the commanders of the fleet the authority to make all decisions during battle.

Philip's plan

The preparation of the Spanish Armada took two years, beginning in 1586. Philip placed Don Alonso Pérez de Guzmán el Bueno, Duke of Medina Sidonia (1550–1615), in command. The duke was an experienced soldier on land, but he had no naval experience. Philip did not share decision-making even with the commander. He mapped out detailed instructions, leaving little room to adapt to circumstances. Medina Sidonia was to set out from the port at Lisbon, Portugal (which Philip had ruled since 1580) with the Armada's 130 ships, carrying nineteen thousand soldiers and eight thousand sailors, as well as arms and supplies for the voyage. The Armada would sail up the English Channel and meet up somewhere along the way with the Duke of Parma's forces. The combined fleet would transport thirty thousand troops from the Netherlands to the English port of Kent. From there they could begin their land invasion under the command of Parma. Philip did not assign a specific place for Parma and Medina Sidonia to meet. The king had faith that, since he was carrying out God's task, God would bring the troops together when the time came.

Naval fighting was not the strength of the Spanish military. The Spanish troops were trained to damage an enemy ship by sailing in close and then shooting it with heavy guns and cannons. Once the damage was inflicted, they were prepared to board and engage in the hand-to-hand combat, in which they excelled. Most of the ships of the Armada were converted merchant ships. They were designed to carry the heavy cargo necessary for long voyages. As a result they were bulky and could not be easily maneuvered.

The Spanish Armada

The Armada set off from Lisbon in May 1588, but several bad storms slowed its progress. On July 29, a storm-battered Armada entered the English Channel. Rather than attacking the English at once, Medina Sidonia gathered his officers to determine what to do. The Duke of Parma had not received word of the Armada's arrival and was six days away from the coast. Most of the ship captains wanted to immediately attack the English fleet, but Philip's instructions did not allow for change, so the Armada formed a defensive crescent shape and proceeded cautiously up the Channel hoping to meet up with Parma.

When the Armada was spotted by one of England's lookouts, the English fleet commanders were hurriedly preparing their ships for battle. According to English legend, Drake was in the middle of a game of bowls, a game similar to bowling that is played on a lawn. After hearing that the powerful Armada was nearby he coolly continued playing to the end of the game, once again demonstrating his fearlessness. The English fleet was ready to sail by nightfall, and by morning they were within sight of the Armada. For the next couple of days the two fleets tested each other's strengths and weaknesses. The Spaniards observed the superiority of English gunnery, and tried to force a closer fight so they could board

When news came that the Spanish Armada was approaching, Francis Drake calmly continued his game of bowls. HULTON ARCHIVE/GETTY IMAGES.

the ships for hand-to-hand combat. The English knew this was what the Spanish planned and kept their distance.

Meanwhile, the Spanish fleet continued up the English Channel. Medina Sidonia wanted to make contact with Parma, so he led his fleet across the Channel and dropped anchor near Calais, France. The English took advantage of the situation. On the night of August 7 they filled eight of their oldest vessels with dry materials, set them on fire, and let the wind propel the burning ships directly into the Spanish fleet. Preloaded guns on the decks of the fire ships discharged in response to the heat of the fire, shooting directly into the Spanish ranks. In a panic, some of the Spanish captains headed for open water. Only after frantic efforts did the Spanish commander bring the fleet back into formation.

The following morning all the available English ships closed in on the Spanish fleet in the fierce, nine-hour Battle of Gravelines. The Spaniards fought well, but the English, with their light warships and superior gunnery, delivered many damaging blows. After a storm brought the fighting to a halt Medina Sidonia considered renewing the battle. Instead he decided to return to Spain to get more supplies. As the Armada sailed around the north of Scotland and then southward off the west coast of Ireland, they encountered unusually violent storms. These storms sank more ships than the English guns had. The survivors of the storms still had to complete the voyage home, during which infectious diseases raged on board the ships. Only 66 of the original 130 ships made it back to Spain, and fewer than half of the thirty thousand men survived the voyage.

The English, facing the same spread of infectious diseases, had followed the Armada only as far as Edinburgh, and then returned to port. Hundreds of English seamen died from disease. The survivors were forced to wait months for their pay from the nearly bankrupted royal treasury. Many English soldiers died of disease or starvation after their success in battle.

The aftermath

On the coasts of England the English people kept watch for a Spanish invasion, not yet knowing the fate of the Armada. By August 18 it was considered safe enough for the queen to ride to Tilbury, where about seventeen thousand men, under the command of Robert Dudley, massed in preparation for the threatened invasion. There the queen delivered one of her most stirring speeches, as quoted in the *Norton Anthology of Literature,* 6th edition:

> I am come amongst you, as you see, at this time, not for my recreation and disport, but being resolved, in the midst and heat of the battle, to live and die amongst you all; to lay down for my God, and for my kingdom, and my people, my honour and my blood, even in the dust. I know I have the body but of a weak and feeble woman; but I have the heart and stomach of a king, and of a king of England too, and think foul scorn that Parma or Spain, or any prince of Europe, should dare to invade the borders of my realm; to which rather than any dishonour shall grow by me, I myself will take up arms. . . .

The English enthusiastically celebrated their victory, which proved that Spain's domination could be stopped and that England had a rightful place among the powers of Europe. Elizabeth's standing as the triumphant queen of England was revered. But most Englishmen understood that their victory could be attributed as much to the weather as to

Elizabeth I gives a rallying speech to her troops at Tilbury.
HULTON ARCHIVE/GETTY IMAGES.

military competence. This nine-day battle would not end the war. In fact Spain and England would continue to battle for fifteen more years, and England won very few victories. England's attempt to invade Spain and Portugal in April 1589 failed miserably. In 1596 Francis Drake and John Hawkins both died after being defeated by the Spanish in Puerto Rico. Spain did little better, however. In 1596 and 1597 Philip used his vast resources to send two fleets greater than the original Armada to invade England but they were, once again, scattered by storms. Until Elizabeth's death England and Spain remained in a stalemate.

For More Information

BOOKS

Hanson, Neil. *The Confident Hope of a Miracle: The True History of the Spanish Armada.* New York: Knopf, 2005.

Martin, Colin and Geoffrey Parker. *The Spanish Armada.* New York: Norton, 1988.

Norton Anthology of Literature. 6th edition, Vol. 1. New York: W. W. Norton, 1993.

Smith, Lacey Baldwin. *The Elizabethan Epic.* London: Panther, 1969.

Weir, Alison. *The Life of Elizabeth I.* New York: Ballantine Books, 1998.

PERIODICALS

McKinnon-Bell, David. "Philip II of Spain: Champion of Catholicism." *History Today,* September 2001, pp. 19–24.

WEB SITES

Adams, Simon. "The Spanish Armada: Church and State, Monarchs and Leaders." *BBC History.* http://www.bbc.co.uk/history/state/ monarchs_leaders/adams_armada_01.shtml (accessed on July 11, 2006).

Alchin, Linda. "The Spanish Armada." *Elizabethan Era.* http:// www.elizabethan-era.org.uk/the-spanish-armada.htm (accessed on July 11, 2006).

Hooker, Richard. "The Wars of Religion." *World Civilizations.* http:// www.wsu.edu/~dee/REFORM/WARS.HTM (accessed on July 11, 2006).

8

A Changing View of the Universe: Philosophy and Science in the Elizabethan Era

By the early sixteenth century the mystery of what lay beyond the three known continents of Europe, Asia, and Africa had been solved. Thanks to the work of brave explorers, the unknown regions, which had previously been described in supernatural terms, were suddenly transformed into concrete world geography. (For more information on exploration, see Chapter 6.) This discovery marked a gradual change in the way European people viewed the universe during the Renaissance, the era beginning around 1350 in Europe, in which scholars turned their attention to classical Greek and Latin learning and shifted to a more rational (based on reason rather than spiritual belief or church authority) approach to philosophy, religion, and science. Historians consider the Renaissance the beginning of the last of three major divisions of European history: the classical or ancient era, during which the Greek and Roman civilizations flourished (c. 500 BCE to c. 500 CE); the Middle Ages, or medieval era, which lasted from c. 500 to c. 1500; and the modern era, which began with the Renaissance and continues to the present. During the Elizabethan Era in England, the period associated with the reign of Queen Elizabeth I (1558–1603) that is often considered to be a golden age in English history, people were in transition between the Middle Ages and modern times.

During the Middle Ages the mysteries of the natural world were viewed as part of God's design. Europeans considered it beyond the capacity of humans to understand these mysteries, and they believed it was wrong and even dangerous to try to control or change the set order of the world. During the Renaissance, however, more and more people accepted secular (non-religious) attempts to understand the natural world. They did not feel that their endeavors conflicted with Christian beliefs; rather, they believed that human learning and accomplishments increased the glory of the God that created them. Many events contributed to this change in worldview. Exploration, the rediscovery of the

WORDS TO KNOW

alchemy: A science of medieval times that attempted to transform base metals into gold and find a potion for eternal life.

angel: A spiritual being ranking superior to humans, but at the lowest level of heavenly beings.

archangel: A spiritual being ranked above the angels.

astrology: The study of the position of stars and planets in the belief that they influence human affairs and events on Earth.

astronomy: The scientific study of the stars, planets, and other celestial bodies.

civic: Relating to the rights and duties of citizens.

classical: Of or relating to the art, literature, architecture and way of life of ancient Greece or Rome, roughly between 500 BCE and 500 CE.

empirical scientist: A scientific researcher who relies on observation and experiments rather than theory.

heliocentric: Relating to the principle that the sun is the center of the solar system, with the planets rotating around it.

humanism: A cultural and intellectual movement during the Renaissance, following the rediscovery of the art and literature of ancient Greece and Rome, that focused on human values, interests, and welfare.

hypothesis: An explanation of natural phenomenon that has not yet been tested; a theory.

scholasticism: An effort to reconcile the teachings of the ancient classical philosophers with medieval Christian theology.

secular: Non-religious.

seraphim: The top level of angels, ranking closest to God.

writings of the ancient Greek and Roman philosophers, new methods of education, the widespread distribution of books due to the development of the printing press, new scientific techniques, increasing trade and commerce, growing cities, and a rising middle class were all contributing factors.

The changing shape of the universe

In ancient and medieval times there was little or no distinction between the disciplines of science, philosophy, and religion. What we call science today was a part of a wider system called philosophy that combined factual, spiritual, and moral knowledge. The medieval model of the universe described below demonstrates this concept.

Medieval scholars adapted the ancient model of the universe that had been described in detail in the second century by the Greek philosopher Claudius Ptolemy (c. 100–c. 178). In the medieval model the universe was usually depicted as a system of spheres. At the center was a stationary, or unmoving, sphere called Earth. The spheres surrounding the Earth were the seven so-called "planets": the moon, Mercury, Venus, the sun, Mars, Jupiter, and Saturn. Beyond the planets was a crystalline (hard and perfectly clear) sphere where the stars existed as fixed objects. Beyond these spheres were the heavens, with progressively higher spheres for the angels (spiritual beings ranking superior to humans, but at the lowest level of heavenly beings), archangels (spiritual beings ranked above angels), and seraphim (the top level of angels, ranking closest to God). God existed outside of the spheres, where he could watch over the entire system. His primary focus, however, was on human beings at the center of the universe. Beyond the realm of God was the end of the universe, which was considered finite (having a definite end).

According to the Christian religion the Earth had become a place of change, corruption, and death after Adam and Eve committed the original sin of eating the forbidden fruit of the tree of knowledge. Medieval people considered everything in the sublunar sphere (located beneath the sphere containing the moon, sun, and planets; Earth) to be mortal, or subject to death, while everything above the sphere of the moon was eternal. The outer spheres rotated around the Earth in a state of perfect harmony, but because of Original Sin, no human being was able to experience this perfection unless he or she reached heaven after death.

In Elizabethan England most people accepted the medieval model of the universe and the moral lesson it conveyed. They had faith in the set order of the universe and feared chaos if the order of things—God's design—was disrupted. Everyone and everything had its assigned role and rank, or degree, in the universe, from the lowest rocks to the highest orders of angels. Evil and misfortune were thought to result when people tried to change their place in this order. English playwright William Shakespeare (1564–1616) expressed this common view in a famous passage of his 1603 play *Troilus and Cressida*:

> . . . The heavens themselves, the planets, and this centre [the Earth]
> Observe degree, priority, and place. . . .
> Take but degree away, untune that string,
> And hark what discord [disharmony] follows.

Source: *The Riverside Shakespeare.* Boston: Houghton Mifflin, 1974, p. 455.

Nicolaus Copernicus's observations of the planets and stars led to his heliocentic theory that the sun is the center of the universe. © BETTMANN/CORBIS.

Although the medieval model of the universe persisted throughout the Renaissance, a new theory about the shape of the universe arose around 1512, when Polish astronomer Nicholaus Copernicus (1473–1543) wrote *De Revolutionibus Orbium Coelestium (Revolution of the Heavenly Spheres)*, explaining his heliocentric theory. This theory held that the Earth, along with the other planets, rotated around the sun. Copernicus had arrived at this theory using mathematics and observation of the stars and planets. Though he was convinced of his findings, he was reluctant to publicize his ideas, since they contradicted the teachings of the church. According to church leaders the Earth was the center of the universe because the humans who lived there were the constant focus of God's divine rule. Copernicus waited more than thirty years to have his work published, but many European astronomers knew of his theories and some continued his work.

The heliocentric model of the universe would not find widespread acceptance until 1609, but by the time Elizabeth took the throne in 1558 people had started to doubt the medieval model. Europeans no longer looked up at the sky with the same certainty that they were looking at the home of the angels. As people began to understand the universe as an infinite (having no end) realm, the human place within it grew increasingly uncertain. Where previously there had been an almost unquestioned belief that all human experiences were part of a divine plan, during the Renaissance many people began to believe in chance: the idea that events occur at random. The individual now felt that he or she had some control over daily life. Elizabethans found a new faith in the power of the individual to unravel the mysteries of the physical world—just as human beings in the early sixteenth century had explored the great unknown areas on the world map. These changes happened very gradually, however; most people during the Elizabethan Era held onto the medieval model of the universe even as they began to adopt a new worldview.

Renaissance education and the rise of humanism

Most scholars in the Middle Ages had been part of a movement called scholasticism, an effort to reconcile the teachings of the ancient classical philosophers with medieval Christian theology. They had rediscovered the works of the Greek philosopher Aristotle (384–322 BCE) during the thirteenth century and followed his example in trying to explain their religion through logic and reason. Medieval universities and monasteries adopted a technique in which a teacher raised a question, usually about an aspect of Christian knowledge that seemed to conflict with ancient philosophy. The students then entered a philosophical debate trying to reconcile Christianity and ancient philosophy through logic.

Scholasticism was gradually replaced with a new form of higher education, called humanism. Humanism is the cultural and intellectual movement during the Renaissance, following the rediscovery of the art and literature of ancient Greece and Rome, that focused on human values, interests, and welfare. The movement began in the city-state of Florence around 1350. The father of humanism, poet and scholar Francesco Petrarch (1304–1374), was frustrated by the scholastics' continual arguing over the fine points of religion. Such debates, he felt, were abstract and not particularly relevant to daily life. Petrach began to collect and study the texts of ancient writers other than Aristotle. The ancients had been more interested in the way humans lived—in learning to live as a good citizen of one's homeland—than in what happened after death. Studying the ancient texts directed readers' focus to moral truths that

The Printing Press Helps Bring Humanism to England

The printing press, a machine that could quickly print copies of text in large quantities, helped spread the values of humanism across Europe during the Renaissance. The early development of the printing press took place in Germany in the mid-fifteenth century. German inventor Johannes Gutenberg (c. 1398–1468) developed the first press to publish a long printed book, the famous Gutenberg Bible, between 1454 and 1456. By 1500 more than one thousand printing presses had been established across Europe, and they had collectively produced more than nine million copies of more than forty thousand separate book titles. For the first time books were readily available to anyone who could read them. Though most early books were religious works, there was also a market for the printed texts of the recently rediscovered Greek and Roman writings.

The printing press arrived in England in 1476, when royal servant and translator William Caxton (c. 1422–c. 1491) established a press in Westminster, a city near London. Because European printers were already selling printed copies of ancient classics in England, Caxton decided to focus on original English works or translations in the vernacular, or everyday language. Caxton's books found a ready market among the nobility and wealthy merchants, and because they were printed in the vernacular, the middle and lower classes were also drawn to

William Caxton reviews a manuscript that has just come off his printing press. Caxton's press helped make humanistic texts readily available in England. © BETTMANN/CORBIS.

them. In his fifteen years as a printer at Westminster, Caxton published more than one hundred titles, helping to bring humanism to England. His works also promoted early English literature, providing a basis for the Elizabethan poets, essayists, and dramatists to come.

could be applied to human life. Petrarch persuaded other scholars to join his search for ancient manuscripts from the early civilizations of Greece and Rome, and widespread interest in classical texts followed.

A new program of education resulted from the study of the classics. First students learned the classical Latin and Greek languages, then studied the classical texts intently in order to learn their moral and civic (relating to the rights and duties of citizens) principles. At universities throughout Europe the earlier emphasis on logic, classification, and philosophical debate gave way to a new focus on moral philosophy, literature, and history. These studies were considered humanistic, focusing on humans rather than religion, and hence the movement came to be called humanism. Though these courses were secular, the people who taught them were usually devout Christians.

Most Renaissance humanists did not limit their knowledge to one branch of learning. The term "Renaissance man" describes an individual whose talents spanned a variety of disciplines. Two of the most famous Italian Renaissance artists, for example, followed several fields of study. Michelangelo (1475–1564) was a remarkable painter and sculptor and also a skilled architect and poet. Leonardo da Vinci (1452–1519) enhanced his artwork by studying mathematics, engineering, and anatomy, the study of the structure of the human body. Though some upper-class Renaissance women were well educated, they were usually not considered men's intellectual equals or given the opportunity to achieve independent fame and fortune. Queen Elizabeth, however, was a ruler, poet, translator, dancer, and musician, and she would certainly fit into the definition of the Renaissance individual.

The first English humanists

The values of humanism spread from Italy to France, Germany, England, and the Netherlands around the end of the fifteenth century. One of the greatest humanist scholars was the Dutch cleric Desiderius Erasmus (1466–1536), who had been trained in a monastery and had taken his orders as a priest. Displeased with the monastery's scholastic approach to education, Erasmus went to Paris to teach. He eventually became a professor of Greek at Cambridge University in England. His best-known writings were about Christianity. Like Petrarch, he believed that scholastics had corrupted the faith, making doctrines too complicated to be useful in everyday life. His book *In Praise of Folly* (1509) is a criticism of the clergy and scholars of his day. In this and many other works he captivated the reading public with his common sense and his practical application of humanist theory to real life. When Martin Luther's (1483–1546) Protestant reforms spread in the 1520s many colleagues thought Erasmus would join the efforts to form a new Christian church. But Erasmus remained a loyal Catholic, believing reforms should be undertaken within the church.

Desiderius Erasmus was one of the most famous humanist scholars. PUBLIC DOMAIN.

Erasmus's good friend, English writer and statesman Thomas More (1478–1535), shared his frustration with the corruption in religion and politics. More's greatest work, *Utopia* (1516), was based on the Greek philosopher Plato's (c. 428–c. 348 BCE) classic work *The Republic,* which attempts to determine the traits of a perfect state. *Utopia* describes an imaginary land noticeably lacking the greed and violence common to Europe. Contrasting contemporary England to the ideal world of his book, More demonstrates a more reasonable way to live, in which the government functions to increase human happiness. Like Erasmus, More had no trouble reconciling his Catholic faith with the teachings of the ancient Greeks.

Humanism during the reign of Henry VIII

Renaissance humanism was popular among educators and scholars in England in the early 1500s—the first decades of King Henry VIII's (1491–1547; reigned 1509–47) rule. The king had been educated by humanists and placed humanist statesmen in high government positions. Thomas More became one of his chief advisors. But in the 1530s Henry VIII broke with the Roman Catholic Church because it would not grant an annulment to his marriage, and created his own English religion. Those who would not comply with his religion were punished or executed. During the remainder of his reign few dared speak freely or honestly about what they believed. Thomas More was an exception. Unable to support the king's actions in breaking with the church, he resigned from his office as the king's advisor. Henry still demanded that More swear an oath rejecting the Roman Catholic pope's authority over the church in England and endorsing the king's right to lead the church in England. More's conscience would not allow him to take the oath, and for his refusal, he was executed in 1535.

During the Middle Ages England's two major universities, Oxford and Cambridge, had been bustling centers of scholasticism, active in the training of young men for careers in the Catholic Church. During the reign of Henry VIII, however, when the Catholic Church was no longer accepted in the kingdom and few dared discuss their beliefs, attendance at the universities dropped greatly and did not pick up again until after the king's death. In the 1550s Oxford and Cambridge once again filled with students. At this time, though, the revived schools were staffed by well-educated humanists, an increasing number of whom were Protestant reformers. Along with the traditional curriculum of liberal arts and philosophy, English universities featured a new focus on the study of Greek and Latin. Students were mainly members of the nobility, and many of them did not intend to enter church-related careers. A university education had become necessary for many other professions, such as serving in Parliament or becoming an officer of the state.

The queen's education

Queen Elizabeth exemplified the transition between medieval times and the Renaissance. For her, as for many others, the new worldview of the Renaissance existed side by side with the well-established views of the Middle Ages. Her understanding of her power as a queen was based on the medieval concept that everyone's role in life had been determined by God and could

Renaissance Medicine

Since the days of Aristotle science had been based on the belief that all of the Earth's matter was made up of four elements: earth, water, air, and fire. Human beings were thought to be microcosms, or little worlds, that were smaller versions of the macrocosm, or the world at large. Thus the four elements of the world were thought to correspond to four humors, or body fluids, in humans. These fluids, which were associated with human characteristics, were believed to exist in a state of balance within the body. The four humors had the following corresponding elements and traits:

- **Blood** corresponded to the element of fire and was associated with a cheerful character.
- **Phlegm (mucus)** corresponded to earth and was associated with a slow, unexcitable nature.
- **Black bile (digestive juices)** corresponded with water and was associated with sadness and depression.
- **Yellow bile** corresponded to air and was associated with anger and bad temper.

Renaissance philosophy held that imbalance in the body's humors resulted in disease. Thus treatments for disease were usually attempts to restore balance by draining off an excess of one of the humors. Elizabethan doctors frequently practiced bloodletting—cutting open a vein to let the blood flow—to cure fevers, infections, and diseases. Sometimes they placed leeches (blood-sucking worms) on prescribed parts of the body to suck out blood. In other cases they induced vomiting. According to modern medicine most of these remedies were harmful, or at least not helpful, to the patient.

In the early Renaissance, some scholars began to study the human body through dissection, cutting the body open in order to examine the organs, and systematic observation. The pioneers of the new science of anatomy were Leonardo da Vinci, whose fascination in the workings of the human body led to masterful sketches of its internal structures, and Belgian anatomist and physician Andreas Vesalius (1514–1564). In 1543 Vesalius wrote a seven-volume text on the structure of the human body illustrated with engravings based on his own drawings. Vesalius rejected the medical theories that had been passed down from the ancient Greeks and Romans. He believed that the only reliable source of information on human anatomy was the close observation of a dissected human corpse. He showed the human body to be composed of internal organs that function together, and his descriptions and drawings were the most accurate study of anatomy ever undertaken up to that time.

not be questioned or changed; she held firmly to this belief throughout her life. Elizabeth's education, though, was based on the new learning of the Renaissance. It fostered within her a lifetime curiosity about astronomy and mathematics, the new geography, and classical philosophy.

As a young girl Elizabeth lived in a royal household at Hatfield, twenty miles north of London. There she, her half-brother Edward

Educator Roger Ascham with Elizabeth I. Elizabeth had invited Ascham to become her personal tutor in 1548. ©
HULTON-DEUTSCH/CORBIS.

(1537–1553), half-sister Mary (1516–1558), and other noble children were educated by England's finest teachers. Most of the royal tutors came from the humanist tradition at Cambridge University, and among them was one of the top Greek scholars in England, Roger Ascham (1515–1568). Ascham had arrived at Cambridge in 1530, just in time to participate in the revolutionary changes brought about by the Renaissance. He remained there as an educator after graduating.

In 1548 Elizabeth invited Ascham to be her personal tutor. Under Ascham's guidance Elizabeth studied languages, religious studies, grammar, logic, mathematics, philosophy, history, penmanship, and music, but Ascham stressed language studies over all else. His method of teaching Elizabeth Greek, Latin, and French languages was to have her translate texts from their original language into English and then to translate her own English translations back into the original language. Elizabeth was an exceptionally good student; she was fluent in six languages by the age of eleven. Ascham took a bold step in instructing her in the art of public speaking, which was a highly unusual subject for a woman at the time. Elizabeth excelled in it.

As a humanist, Ascham believed that education's purpose was to provide a practical guide to living a moral life. Though we cannot know the extent of his effect on the future queen, a comparison of Elizabeth and her father, Henry VIII, shows a widely different view of the monarch's responsibility. While Henry viewed his every whim as divinely ordained, Elizabeth carefully crafted her public image and her actions to try to meet her civic responsibility. One of the things Ascham valued most was style, or speaking, writing, and comporting oneself with intelligence and elegance. This emphasis on style was fundamental to Elizabeth's reign as queen of England, and undoubtedly influenced her court and the culture of her land.

John Dee, mathematician, astrologer, and magician

In Elizabethan England people did not distinguish between astronomy, the scientific study of the stars and planets, and astrology, the study of the influence of the stars and planets on human life. Most accepted that the positions of the planets and stars determined human fate. In 1558, when it was time for Elizabeth to choose the day of her coronation, or crowning as queen, she turned to astrology to find the most favorable day. She selected as her astrologer John Dee (1527–1608). Dee was not only a respected astrologer, but also a scholar, mathematician, astronomer, ancient text collector, geographer, and author. Dee was a true example of a Renaissance man in England.

Dee was a brilliant student who, at the age of fifteen, studied Greek, Latin, philosophy, geometry, arithmetic, and astronomy at Cambridge University, finishing his degree in just two years. In 1547 he studied with the famed mapmaker Gerardus Mercator (1512–1594) in Belgium. (For more information on Mercator, see Chapter 6.) He would later use his mathematical skills and knowledge of mapmaking to instruct English sailors on geometry and navigation prior to their voyages to the New World. Dee was an excellent mathematician. He drew large crowds to hear him in Paris when he spoke about the Greek mathematician Euclid's (c. 325–c. 260 BCE) principles of geometry.

Dee compiled a huge library of more than four thousand ancient and scholarly books. It was possibly the largest library in Europe at the time. Among his books Dee was most fascinated with those dealing with the supernatural. He was particularly interested in the symbols, language, and numbers used in communicating with the spirit world. He became absorbed in trying to find the pure language that had been used at the beginning of life on Earth, as well as magic numbers that could tap into the powers of the universe. He became absorbed in the supernatural, and soon rumors spread throughout England that he was a witch or black magician. Dee's purpose, though, was to find the ultimate truths about the universe. A Christian, he believed that God's power was beyond human understanding, but he sought to find the ways that divine power worked in the natural world, believing it was possible for humans to draw upon that power.

During his early years, Dee wrote two books that explored the power of the stars and planets to influence events in the human world—that is, to scientifically explain astrology. His work was equally devoted to astronomy. A new star appeared in the skies around 1572, bringing great fear to Europeans who thought it might be an evil omen. Dee studied it empirically, through scientific investigation, and accurately determined its distance from Earth using advanced mathematics. Queen Elizabeth was impressed with his skills, and asked him to advise her and teach her mathematics. However, she did not give him financial support, and Dee struggled with poverty throughout his life.

Dee is often remembered for the work of his later years. By 1581, certain that spirits were trying to communicate with him, he began gazing into a crystal ball, hoping to make contact with the supernatural world. A man named Edward Kelley convinced Dee that he could talk with angels. Dee gave Kelley a crystal ball and soon Kelley was relaying the messages of the angels to Dee, who recorded them. The two men wrote a book about their communications and the language used by the angels. This late period, during which Dee was reportedly communicating with the angels and practicing alchemy, a science of medieval times that attempted to transform base metals into gold and find a potion for eternal life, led later historians to dismiss his efforts as unscientific. But Dee's search for the

Alchemy

Alchemy was one of the most popular sciences of the Renaissance. At its most basic form, alchemy was the attempt to find the philosopher's stone, a stone or substance that could turn base metals, such as lead, into gold. For some, this pursuit was simply an effort to find great wealth, but for others, the ancient science of alchemy was actually far more complex, combining natural philosophy, metallurgical arts (the science of metals), and magic. True alchemists believed that if they could find the purifying agent that refined lead into gold, they could use the same substance or process to transform other matter into its perfect form. In trying to understand how metals develop within the Earth and their evolution toward perfection (gold), alchemists sought to understand the powers of divine creation in the natural world. In this way, alchemy was a kind of scientific exploration of God's work. Some Renaissance scientists pursued alchemy as a branch of medicine, seeking to find a process of purification, that could be practiced on humans. The end result would be perfection, or eternal life.

An alchemist at work in his laboratory. © BETTMANN/ CORBIS.

Most people viewed alchemy with awe and fear. They believed that to change the nature of metals was a disruption of the set order of the universe, since it moved beings from a low degree to a higher one. Interfering in God's creation was considered magic, but it was also considered science; in fact, science and magic were almost indistinguishable concepts in the Middle Ages and Renaissance. One university in Poland even offered an advanced degree in black magic. Nonetheless, magicians were often suspected of causing the world's problems. Scientists and mathematicians were viewed with suspicion as well.

Though alchemy is considered highly unscientific today, some of the top alchemists of the past were pioneers in the fields of chemistry and modern medicine. Perhaps the greatest alchemist, Swiss physician Philippus Aureolus Paracelsus (1493–1541) used knowledge from his alchemy experiments to develop successful chemical drug treatments for disease. Although his interest was in magic, astrology, and alchemy, Paracelsus was an empirical scientist. (An empirical scientist is one who relies on observation and experimental methods.) He contributed significantly to the development of medicine. Later scientists, including English physicist Isaac Newton (1642–1727), also experimented with alchemy.

truth is a remarkable story of the exploration of the universe and its powers based on the existing philosophy of his times.

Thomas Harriot, mathematician and astronomer

Mathematician and scientist Thomas Harriot (1560–1621) was among the next generation of Elizabethan scientists. After taking his degree at Oxford University, Harriot was employed in 1584 by statesman and poet Walter Raleigh (1552–1618) as household accountant and the designer of Raleigh's ships. When Raleigh organized his first expedition to establish a colony in the New World, Harriot instructed its seamen in methods of navigation. The expedition returned, carrying two natives named Manteo and Wanchese, who had been kidnapped in the colony of Roanoke off the coast of what is now North Carolina. Harriot spent time with the two natives, learning their language and creating an alphabet so he could write it down. The following year Raleigh sent a second expedition to settle a colony in the New World. Harriot accompanied the group as the scientist and historian of the expedition. While sailing to the New World, Harriot observed and recorded a solar eclipse with remarkable accuracy. At the Roanoke colony Harriot worked with artist John White (died c. 1593), studying the native people, vegetation, animal life, and other natural resources. He published *A Briefe and True Report,* an account of his findings, in 1588. It was the first book in English to describe the New World. Among its many merits, the book served as a foundation of the science of anthropology. (Anthropology is the study of human beings, particularly in reference to their cultures, environment, physical characteristics, and origins.)

After returning to England Harriot continued his scientific observations of the natural universe, first with the financial support of Raleigh, and later under Henry Percy, Earl of Northumberland (1564–1632). In his early thirties he began working in astronomy and optics, the study of light. Harriot studied the way light bent when it passed through a glass or through liquid, discovering the law of refraction (the bending of light). He is credited with being the first person in England to build and use a telescope. He used his telescope to draw some of the earliest maps of the moon's surface. He also observed Jupiter's moons, studied sunspots, dark spots that sometimes appear on the surface of the sun, and calculated the speed of the sun's rotation. Harriot considered many practical problems in his work, such as the flight of cannon shells in order to improve their accuracy. He even investigated specific gravity, the density of a substance compared to the density of water, and developed tables of the specific gravity of various materials. He never published any of his findings and is rarely credited for them.

Harriot is probably best known as a mathematician. He wrote an algebra textbook that was widely used for many years. In this book he developed a number of equations and notations that simplified algebra. He become the first mathematician to use the greater than (>) and less than (<) symbols, and he was one of the first to adopt the plus sign (+) and minus sign (-), lowercase letters for variables, and the equal sign (=).

Sir Francis Bacon, philosopher of science

Francis Bacon (1561–1626) was a statesman, lawyer, writer, philosopher, and scientist. During the reign of Elizabeth he was involved in many political schemes. Though he fell from the queen's favor for a time, by the end of her life he had proved his keen intelligence, and he went on to a more promising career in the reign of James I (1566–1625; reigned 1603–25).

Bacon is probably best remembered for his ambitious plan to revise the methods of science. His scientific approach, often called the Baconian method, was to study the natural world empirically, through collection of data, experimentation, observation, and testing hypotheses. (A hypothesis is an explanation of natural phenomenon that has not yet been tested; a theory). Bacon believed that science had not advanced because it was based on false theories—such as alchemy, the four humors, and the shape of the universe—derived from Aristotle and Plato. He believed that science should be based on the observation of nature and a process of reasoning developed out of such observation. He promoted a practical view of science as a discipline that could improve the quality of human life and eventually help humans to conquer nature. His philosophy of science greatly influenced the next generation of scientists, and spawned the Scientific Revolution, a period of major scientific change that took place in the seventeenth century.

For More Information

BOOKS

Aston, Margaret, ed. *The Panorama of the Renaissance.* London: Thames and Hudson, 1996.

Sir Francis Bacon devised the Baconian method of scientific study, which focused on the empirical study of the natural world. PUBLIC DOMAIN.

Kirkpatrick, Robin. *The European Renaissance, 1400–1600.* Harlow, England: Pearson Education, 2002.

The Riverside Shakespeare. Boston: Houghton Mifflin Company, 1974.

Wightman, W. P. D. *Science in a Renaissance Society.* London: Hutchinson University Library, 1972.

Woolley, Benjamin. *The Queen's Conjurer: The Science and Magic of Dr. John Dee, Adviser to Queen Elizabeth I.* New York: Henry Holt and Company, 2001.

WEB SITES

Kreis, Steven. "Renaissance Humanism." *The History Guide: Lectures on Modern European Intellectual History.* http://www.historyguide.org/intellect/humanism.html (accessed on July 11, 2006).

"The Renaissance Connection" (interactive). *Allentown Art Museum.* http://www.renaissanceconnection.org/main.cfm (accessed on July 11, 2006).

"The Spell Binder." http://www.channel4.com/science/microsites/S/spellbinder/index.shtml (accessed on July 11, 2006).

9

The Arts in the Elizabethan World

During the early Renaissance, an era spanning from the fourteenth century to the seventeenth century, the arts in Europe blossomed into bold new forms, blending the philosophy and creative forms of the ancient civilizations of Rome and Greece with contemporary European style. (For more information on the Renaissance, see Chapter 8.) England, separated from the European continent by the English Channel and caught up in religious upheaval during the fifteenth century, was slow to respond to the new artistic influences of the Renaissance. It was not until the Elizabethan Era, the period associated with the reign of Queen Elizabeth I (1558–1603) that is often considered to be a golden age in English history, that the English Renaissance began.

Elizabethan artists drew from European Renaissance ideals, but they also brought a unique national sensibility to their work. Among the many influences on their style was Elizabeth herself. Her image was often invoked in painting and literature, and her appreciation of music, dancing, and pageantry raised them to a higher level of artistry. (A pageant is a dramatic presentation, such as a play, that often depicts a historical, biblical, or traditional event.) Like most English people, though, Elizabeth did not distinguish much between popular entertainment and the higher arts. She was as happy to watch a bearbaiting (a form of entertainment in which a bear is tied to a post and attacked by dogs in front of spectators) or view a fireworks display as to listen to her court musicians perform or attend a play.

In modern times we tend to think of art as the expression of the artist's deepest feelings and beliefs. This was not true in Elizabeth's day. All English artists were expected to fulfill their patriotic duty by glorifying the queen. Since it was impossible in the Elizabethan age to support oneself through art, most artists depended on patrons (wealthy sponsors who helped them financially), and they frequently flattered potential patrons in their art, hoping for financial reward. There was no right to

WORDS TO KNOW

allegory: A story or painting that represents abstract ideas or principles as characters, figures, or events.

alliteration: Repetition of the same consonant at the beginning of words or syllables.

chiaroscuro: In drawing or painting, a method of depicting depth and space by contrasting light and dark and creating shadows.

courtier: A person who serves or participates in the royal court or household as the king's or queen's advisor, officer, or attendant.

epic: A long poem that relates the deeds of a hero and is of particular importance to a culture or nation.

fresco: A painting done on wet plaster.

iconoclasm: The deliberate destruction of religious icons (sacred images, statues, objects, and monuments) usually for religious or political reasons.

lute: A plucked string instrument similar to a guitar but shaped like a pear, with six to thirteen strings and a deep round back.

madrigal: A polyphonic love song for four to six voices without musical accompaniment.

martyr: A person who chooses to be punished or put to death rather than to abandon his or her religious beliefs.

meter: The pattern of stressed and unstressed syllables in poetry.

monopoly: The exclusive right to trade with a particular market or group of markets.

nationalism: Patriotism and loyalty to a person's own country.

pageant: A dramatic presentation, such as a play, that often depicts a historical, biblical, or traditional event.

patron: Someone who financially sponsors, or supports, an artist, entertainer, or explorer.

perspective: An artistic technique used to make a two-dimensional (flat) representation appear to be three-dimensional by considering how the objects within the picture relate to one another.

polyphony: Music with many voices; or the mixing together of several melodic lines at the same time in a musical composition.

progress: A royal procession, or trip, made by a monarch and a large number of his or her attendants.

prose: Ordinary speech or writing; not poetry.

retinue: Group of attendants.

rhyme scheme: The pattern of rhymes in a poem.

romance: A literary work about improbable events involving characters that are quite different from ordinary people.

saint: A deceased person who, due to his or her exceptionally good behavior during life, receives the official blessing of the church and is believed to be capable of interceding with God to protect people on earth.

simile: A comparison between unlike things usually using the words "like" or "as".

stanza: A group of lines that form a section of a poem.

symmetrical: Balanced, with the same-sized parts on each side.

virginal: A small, legless, and rectangular keyboard instrument related to the harpsichord.

free speech or freedom of the press in Elizabethan England, and it was very dangerous to write, paint, or even sing directly about the issues of the day. Artists and writers often found indirect ways to represent contemporary problems. Most used the ancient art of allegory, a story or painting that represents abstract ideas or principles as characters, figures, or events. Some writers wrote about historical events of the distant past that were similar enough to current events that audiences understood the author was presenting these events as commentary on current social problems.

Visual arts of the Renaissance

In the Middle Ages (c. 500–c. 1500; the period of European history between ancient times and the Renaissance) most Europeans considered the arts to be a means of conveying religious ideas. Paintings, frescoes (paintings done on wet plaster), tapestries, and stained-glass windows were created to show stories or figures from the Bible. Religious art was particularly useful at a time when the majority of the population could not read but could recognize a biblical story in pictures. As the Renaissance began in Europe in the late fourteenth century, however, artists began to turn away from religious themes. With the new study of ancient Greek and Roman texts, the focus became more secular (non-religious), emphasizing the glory of human beings and the natural world around them. Figures from ancient mythology, or traditional stories featuring Greek and Roman gods and heroes, were mixed with traditional Christian themes.

In technique, too, Renaissance paintings differed from medieval ones. The earlier paintings looked flat because the artists lacked the techniques of perspective and chiaroscuro (kee-ahr-aw-SKEW-roh) that arose in the Renaissance. Perspective is an artistic technique used to make a two-dimensional (flat) representation appear to be three-dimensional by considering how the objects within the picture relate to one another. For example, in a painting, objects meant to be seen as farther away are depicted as smaller and higher than objects meant to be seen as closer to the viewer. Chiaroscuro is a method of depicting depth and space by contrasting light and dark and creating shadows. (*Chiaro* means "light" in Italian, and *oscuro* means "dark".)

English painting

The first artistic influence of the Renaissance arrived in England when Henry VIII brought in some of the finest painters from Europe in the

Hans Holbein the Younger brought realistic, secular painting to England. KEAN COLLECTION/GETTY IMAGES.

early decades of the sixteenth century. Foremost among them was Hans Holbein the Younger (c. 1487–1543) from Germany, who painted portraits of Henry's courtiers and brought realistic, secular portrait painting to England. (Courtiers are people who serve or participate in the royal court or household as the king's advisor, officer, or attendant.) By Elizabeth's reign portrait painting was the most common type of painting in the nation. Elizabethan portraits are notable for their close attention to

The Reformation and the Arts

In 1521 the teachings of Martin Luther (1483–1546) started the Protestant Reformation (also known as the Reformation; a sixteenth-century religious movement that aimed to reform the Roman Catholic Church and resulted in the establishment of Protestant churches). In the decades that followed many northern European countries, such as the German states, the Netherlands, England, and Scotland, adopted Protestantism, while southern European states, such as Italy, France, and Spain, remained Catholic. The arts developed differently in Catholic and Protestant regions.

Catholics believed that human beings needed the assistance of intermediaries, or go-betweens, to help them communicate with God. The church itself served as an intermediary, but Catholics could also pray to saints, or deceased people who, due to exceptionally good behavior during life, receive the official blessing of the church and are believed to be capable of interceding with God to protect people on earth. Catholic art focused on religious figures in the belief that they brought the viewer closer to God. Catholic churches and homes were usually supplied with many objects of worship. These objects included images and statues of saints and the Virgin Mary, crucifixes, candles, and rosary beads. Most of the Protestant churches, on the other hand, were

simple in design and used few decorations. The Protestants believed that the Bible was the only authority a Christian needed. They considered objects of worship idolatrous—that is, they believed they were wrong because they encouraged worship of something other than God. Protestant leaders such as the French theologian John Calvin (1509–1564) denounced Catholic art as idolatrous and called for the destruction of Catholic images and other artworks.

Destruction of Catholic arts in England began during the reign of Elizabeth's father, Henry VIII (1491–1547), when he closed down the Catholic monasteries, or houses for monks who live under religious vows. During the reign of Elizabeth's Protestant younger brother, Edward VI (1537–1553), a movement called iconoclasm began. (Iconoclasm is the deliberate destruction of religious icons: sacred images, statues, objects, and monuments.) Protestant mobs attacked the Catholic churches in England, destroying paintings, statues, tapestries, altars, and stained-glass windows. A second iconoclast movement took place soon after Elizabeth took the throne, much to the new queen's disapproval. Elizabeth loved some of the arts of the Catholic religion. Though she was unable to completely stop the iconoclast movement in England, she played a strong role in preserving some of the art and music of the Catholic Church.

the elaborate costumes of their subjects as well as the richly detailed background.

Upper-class Elizabethans loved portrait-miniatures. These were tiny, but highly detailed, painted portraits, some as small as two inches high. The portrait-miniature was a uniquely English contribution to the Renaissance, and Nicholas Hilliard (1547–1619) was the master of the art. Hilliard painted his first miniature of the queen in 1572. She is wearing an elaborate black dress with white embroidered sleeves, a white rose pinned to her shoulder, and a small frill ruff. Ruffs were the highly starched circular collars worn by Elizabethan men and women, either attached to the clothing or as a separate garment. Brightly colored gold lettering surrounds the queen's head. The miniature is painted in watercolor on the back of a playing card, the queen of hearts.

Hilliard's talent for lifelike representation of the physical world is obvious in his detailed depictions of Elizabethan clothing. He invented many new methods of painting the details of his subjects' costumes, including the fabrics, metals, and jewels. For example, he portrayed the starched crispness of lace ruffs by painting the complicated lace patterns with a brush loaded with white lead. When the lead-loaded paint dried the lace patterns stood up in relief. He used real gold and silver in his paint, polished with a small animal tooth to create tiny, perfect surfaces of gleaming metal. To represent diamonds he drew and shaded the cut of the stone with transparent black and gray over polished silver. Hilliard was also highly skilled at capturing his subjects' character and appearance. It is largely thanks to him that we know what leading figures of Elizabethan days—such as poet and statesman Walter Raleigh (1522–1618); explorer Francis Drake (c. 1540–1596), and statesman Robert Dudley (Earl of Leicester; 1532–1588)—actually looked like.

Hilliard, like other painters of the queen, was not allowed to create a lifelike portrait of her. Elizabeth was very careful about her public image. Her ministers hired a few select painters to paint her portrait. These artists created patterns, or examples of the look that was acceptable to the royal court, and the patterns were then distributed to other appointed painters to copy. The queen's portraits provided the regal image of a powerful monarch, the steady, never-aging force behind England. They probably do not reflect what she actually looked like. Those painted when Elizabeth was in her sixties, for example, do not show the wrinkles and chalky face make-up, the loss of her hair, or the blackening of her teeth that written descriptions of her noted.

Hilliard and his student, Isaac Oliver (c. 1560–1617), made miniatures very popular in Elizabethan times. Other artists, such as Robert Peake the Elder (died 1619), Marcus Gheeraerts the Younger (1561–1635), and George Gower (1540–1596), made large, full-length paintings that portray the noble class in richly adorned costumes complete with armor, embroidery, ruffs, hunting gear, weapons, and lace.

A portrait of Elizabeth I by Nicholas Hilliard. © FRANCIS G. MAYER/CORBIS.

Architecture

In medieval times much of England's finest architecture had been devoted to its churches and cathedrals, but church-building came to a halt during Henry VIII's reign, after his break with the Catholic Church.

Longleat House is one Robert Smythson's most famous architectural creations. © CLAY PERRY/CORBIS.

In Elizabeth's reign architecture took on a new importance as the growing class of wealthy courtiers began to build huge homes called "great houses" or "prodigy houses" in rural areas of England. Most summers Elizabeth took trips called progresses around the English countryside, usually traveling with a retinue, or group of attendants, of about five hundred people. She and her full retinue lodged at the great houses of her courtiers, and the hosts were expected to feed, house, and entertain this huge group of guests. Though the queen's visits were extremely expensive, they were considered a great honor to the host. Competition grew among courtiers to build bigger and more elaborate country estates.

The homes of the wealthy had previously been built around court-yards so they could be defended against enemy attacks. Elizabethan country houses, however, were open to their surroundings. They were symmetrical, or balanced, with the same-sized parts on each side. Most were built in the shape of a letter H or a letter E. In a letter E house, the long line of the E was a great hall on the bottom floor, used mainly for showing off expensive art and impressing visitors. The lines at either end of the E were respectively the kitchen and living quarters. The shorter line in the middle was an entrance porch. On the upper floor, above the great hall, was a long gallery that ran the full length of the house and was used for entertaining and for daily family life. Most of the great houses were made of stone.

In Elizabethan times there were no professional architects to design buildings. Usually the owner of the house created his own design or found a design to copy and then hired someone to carry out the construction. Nevertheless, the design of some of the largest and most elaborate sixteenth-century great houses can be attributed to a stonemason named Robert Smythson (1535–1614). One of his most famous works is the enormous house called Longleat in Wiltshire, which was finished in 1580 and is considered one of the finest examples of Elizabethan architecture.

In the cities of Elizabethan England, another common style of house evolved for merchants and the growing middle class. The exterior of the house was black and white with dark wood beams and white clay walls. The bottom floor of the city home was usually a shop or place of business, while the upper floors, which overhung the lower floors and had more room, were the living quarters for the family.

Music

Elizabeth was an accomplished musician, playing the lute (a plucked string instrument similar to a guitar but shaped like a pear, with six to thirteen strings and a deep round back) and the virginal (a small, legless, rectangular keyboard instrument related to the harpsichord) as well as composing her own music. As queen, Elizabeth supported music of all kinds, from popular songs to church music. She kept about seventy musicians in the royal court, and she expected her courtiers to sing, play musical instruments, and dance with grace and ability.

In the first decades of Elizabeth's rule English music was undergoing important changes. Various new musical instruments—the early violin, the harpsichord and virginal, the oboe (a reed instrument), and others—were being used in combination to produce complex sounds. This type of musical arrangement was called polyphony, which means many voices, or

An Elizabethan woman playing the virginal. HULTON ARCHIVE/GETTY IMAGES.

the mixing together of several melodic lines at the same time. Another notable change was the expression of passion and mood in Elizabethan music, which usually highlighted the emotions of the words being sung with the music.

Religious music

The Protestant movement had called for an end to sacred music that evoked Catholic traditions, particularly songs with lyrics (words) in the Latin language. But Elizabeth was particularly fond of the traditional church music and quietly struggled against these prohibitions. Thus it came about that the great master of Elizabethan music was a Catholic composer named William Byrd (c. 1543–1623), who was hired by Elizabeth to a position in the royal chapel in the early 1570s. There he worked with Thomas Tallis (c. 1505–1585), a long-time royal musician and composer. Byrd was looked upon with suspicion by many because of his religion. Elizabeth, though, loved his traditional music and was not concerned about his beliefs. In 1575 she granted Byrd and Tallis a monopoly (the exclusive right to trade with a particular market or group of markets) over printing music in England. The first serious music to be published in England was their *Cantiones Sacrae,* a collection of Latin motets, choral compositions usually sung in Latin and traditionally a part of the Catholic Mass. Though the English public found the collection too Catholic in its sound, these works are today considered some of the greatest Elizabethan compositions, full of intense emotion and musical complexity.

Secular music

Byrd also played a large role in developing the English madrigal, a polyphonic love song for four to six voices without musical accompaniment. The madrigal had once been highly popular in Italy but it had gone out of style there. In England it gained great popularity during Elizabeth's reign, as composers set poetry written in the English language to madrigal musical compositions.

Thomas Campion (1567–1620) was both a poet and a musician, as well as a scientist and physician. He contributed greatly to Elizabethan music with his 119 songs for voice and lute. The songs, called ayres, were about love, death, and beauty. Campion wrote both the lyrics and the music of his songs, masterfully connecting them so that his simple melodies reflected the emotions of his words. Composer John Dowland (1563–1626) also wrote highly popular secular lute songs that balanced beautiful lyrics and instrumental music.

Elizabethan literature

During Elizabeth's reign England experienced its highest level of literacy, the ability to read and write. This was in part due to the great rise in education. (For more information on Elizabethan education, see Chapter 11.) It was also due to the Protestant belief in individual reading and interpretation of the Bible, which made it desirable for everyone to have the ability to read. The development of the printing press also changed the nature of reading and writing in England, making literature widely available to English readers. The universities, too, took on a new focus, educating a large new class of non-religious statesmen and merchants

Puritans and the Arts in Elizabethan England

Many wealthy Protestants had gone into exile in Europe during the reign of the Catholic Mary I (1516–1558). Some had met the followers of John Calvin, who had set up a strict Protestant government in Geneva, Switzerland. These English exiles adopted some of Calvin's more extreme doctrines, and many came to believe that the Bible was to be read literally. According to the Calvinists, a pious person should reject anything that is not specifically discussed in the Bible and follow precisely anything that was mentioned within its pages.

Upon returning to England the Calvinists were dismayed to find that Elizabeth's religious settlement permitted many elements of Roman Catholicism, such as the wearing of vestments (ceremonial robes) by the clergy, the use of the sign of the cross, playing an organ to present church music (rather than the voices of the congregation), and decorating churches with religious ornaments. The radical Protestants desired to "purify" the Church of England of its Roman Catholic customs. The Anglicans, or members of the Church of England, began to call these reformers Puritans, making fun of their rigid piety and self-righteousness.

In Elizabethan times there was no such thing as religious tolerance. It was widely accepted that in order to have a peaceful nation, everyone must believe the same thing. In their intense dedication to their faith, Puritans were unwilling to accept the ways of others. They believed their way had been sanctioned by God. They opposed many things that others valued, such as certain forms of art, instrumental music in church, certain manners of dress, and many popular festivals and pastimes, especially the English theater. Elizabeth, though Protestant, distrusted the Puritans and fought against their attempts to limit music, ban holidays, and close theaters.

who were able to express their views in increasingly sophisticated English prose. (Prose is ordinary speech or writing; not poetry.) Widespread reading and writing was a major force behind the English Renaissance.

Most early Renaissance writers in England strove to imitate the style of the classics. Many continued to write in Latin, the language used for most literary works in England. Others, though, sought to follow in the footsteps of the medieval English author Geoffrey Chaucer (c. 1342–1400), whose poetic work, *The Canterbury Tales,* had been written in English. Like Chaucer, many Elizabethan writers wished to raise the English language, long considered a rough means of expression, to the level of art.

Foxe's *Book of Martyrs*

In the 1530s Mary I took the throne and began persecuting Protestants for their beliefs. By this time Protestant educator and writer John Foxe

(1516–1587) was already writing a book about Protestant martyrs, or people who choose to be punished or put to death rather than to abandon their religious beliefs. He was forced to flee England to avoid persecution. During his exile in Europe, he added to his book the stories he was hearing from England about the torture and execution of Protestants under Mary. His accounts were exciting and featured exaggerated and shocking details. His book was first published under the long title *Acts and Monuments of these latter and perilous days, touching matters of the church, wherein are comprehended and described the great persecution and horrible troubles that have been wrought and practices by the Romish prelates from the year of Our Lord a thousand to the time now present,* but it is often called simply *Book of Martyrs.* It was an enormous, well-illustrated book of more than two thousand pages.

Though Foxe's book was extremely expensive, it became an Elizabethan bestseller, selling more than ten thousand copies by the end of the century. Its strong anti-Catholic sentiments appealed to Protestants, but it was probably its nationalism, or patriotism and loyalty to England, that caught the public attention. The *Book of Martyrs* was one of the first books that presented England, with its own strong Protestant identity, as the center of true Christianity. In 1570 the Church of England ordered all major churches in the nation to purchase a copy.

Debate between Anglicans and Puritans

By the 1580s some of England's finest prose was devoted to the debate between the Anglicans and the Puritans. An anonymous Puritan author using the name Martin Marprelate issued several extremely well argued pamphlets ridiculing the Anglican church and its bishops. The church in turn hired some noted writers to respond to the Marprelate tracts, fueling a war of words between moderate Protestants and Puritan reformers. The debate was temporarily silenced when the printer of the Marprelate pamphlets was arrested and hanged for his part in their publication.

The most acclaimed Elizabethan writer of nonfiction prose was Richard Hooker (1554–1600), a clergyman in the Church of England and an educator in a law school. He began his masterpiece, the eight-volume *Of the Laws of Ecclesiastical Polity* (1593–1597) in response to an argument he was having with a Puritan educator in his school. The Puritan argued that the Bible was the only authority to guide Christians, and that therefore a church led by the queen and her appointed bishops was not right. Hooker argued that along with the

John Stubbs's Right Hand

In 1579 the forty-five-year-old Elizabeth began a courtship with a French prince, the Duke of Alençon (1555–1584). Many English people, particularly the Puritans, were horrified at the prospect of a match with the French royalty, particularly because the Catholic French government had recently been responsible for a large-scale massacre of the French Protestants called the Huguenots. Among the many protests that arose was a popular pamphlet written by a well-respected Puritan named John Stubbs (c. 1543–1591). The pamphlet compared Alençon's presence in England to the devil's presence in the garden of Eden as described in the Old Testament. In Stubbs's argument, the French prince meant to seduce Elizabeth as Satan had seduced Eve with the forbidden apple, destroying the purity of England forever. The pamphlet found an eager audience throughout England.

Stubbs's pamphlet infuriated Elizabeth. Stubbs was arrested, and Elizabeth appealed to the courts to have him and his publisher hanged. The judges, however, did not think the offense was serious enough to be punished by death. Instead, Stubbs and the publisher were to have their right hands cut off before being sent to jail. This punishment was executed at a public platform at Whitehall Palace in London. The executioner chopped off Stubbs's right hand and cauterized (burned) it with a hot iron to stop the bleeding. When this was done, Stubbs put on his hat with his left hand, cried out "God Save the Queen!" and then fainted from pain.

Elizabeth came to regret her harsh actions. Stubbs was released from prison and soon became a member of Parliament, England's legislative body. The message for all writers, however, was clear. It was *extremely* dangerous to anger the queen.

Bible, God had created human beings with the ability to reason, and that this God-given reason could be considered a source of authority. He went on to discuss the place of human beings in the universe and in relation to God, defending the Church of England as the product of human understanding of the divine and natural worlds. Hooker's prose was simple, clear, and elegant as he handled complex philosophical points.

Prose fiction

One of the most influential and popular prose writers of the era was John Lyly (1554–1606). His romances *Euphues, or the Anatomy of Wit* (1578) and its sequel *Euphues and His England* (1580) were published to instant success. (Romances are literary works about improbable events involving characters that are quite different from ordinary people.) Lyly's prose style in these two early romances was called euphuism, named after Lyly's character Euphues. Like the prose of the ancient Greeks and Romans, euphuism featured extremely elaborate sentences, full of similes (comparisons between unlike things usually using the words "like" or "as") and alliteration, or repetition of the same consonant at the beginning of words or syllables. It also included many references to the classics and mythology. Lyly's *Anatomy of Wit* is about two friends who both love the same woman, and come to realize that the bond of friendship is more important than romantic love. An example of the euphuistic language in that book, quoted from the *Internet Shakespeare Editions,* demonstrates the style:

> Time draweth wrinkles in a fair face, but addeth fresh colors to a fast friend, which neither heat, nor cold, nor misery, nor place, nor destiny can alter or diminish. O friendship, of all things the most rare, and therefore most rare because most excellent, whose comfort in misery is always sweet, and whose counsels in prosperity are ever fortunate!

Lyly's prose style was imitated by many Elizabethans, and *Euphues* was praised as an attempt to elevate the English language to a new level of artistic expression. Euphuism, though, quickly became dated and its elegant style was often ridiculed in later literature.

Philip Sidney

In the greatest work of literary criticism of the Elizabethan Era, *The Defence of Poetry* (1595), Philip Sidney (1554–1586) commented that, aside from the writings of Chaucer and a couple of contemporary writers, English literature had never been very good. Although France and Italy and even Scotland had their notable poets, according to Sidney the art of England had "fallen to be the laughing-stock of children." Sidney and a few of his associates were about to change all that, however.

Sidney was a perfect example of an aspiring courtier in Elizabeth's court. His father was a well-connected statesman serving the queen and his uncle was Robert Dudley (Earl of Leicester; 1532–1588), the queen's long-time favorite. In 1575, after traveling extensively in Europe, the bright and handsome young man established himself in Elizabeth's court. He probably would have taken his place there as a favorite had he not gotten himself into trouble by writing to Elizabeth in 1580 to advise her not to marry the Duke of Alençon. The letter infuriated Elizabeth and she immediately banished him from court. Sidney retreated to the home of his sister, Mary Herbert, Countess of Pembroke (1561–1621). Mary was an accomplished writer herself, and gathered the top poets of the country at her estate. In her home Sidney wrote his most famous works, such as

Philip Sidney criticized English literature in Defense of Poetry.

the prose romance *Arcadia,* and *The Defence of Poetry.* He also wrote his highly acclaimed sonnet sequence (a collection of related sonnets) *Astrophil and Stella,* which sparked a revolution in English poetry and literature.

Critics regard *Astrophil and Stella* as Sidney's masterpiece. It is a variation on the Italian sonnet, a form perfected by Italian poet Francesco Petrarch (1304–1374), and was the first sonnet sequence in English literature. The work consists of 110 sonnets written from the perspective of Astrophil, a poet and courtly lover. Astrophil describes his unrequited

Sonnets

There are two major types of sonnets: Italian and English. Sonnets originated in Italy around 1200. The form was later perfected by Italian poet Francesco Petrarch with his famous poems about his unrequited (not returned) love for a married woman named Laura. Most Italian sonnets expressed themes of love and followed a set form. They were fourteen lines long, with the first eight lines setting out a problem and the last six lines resolving it. There was usually a major change in the tone, or the mood of the poem, at the eighth or ninth line. Sonnets contained careful rhyme schemes, or the patterns of rhymes in a poem. The first eight lines of an Italian sonnet rhymed in an *abbaabba* pattern, meaning that the last word of the lines designated as "a" all rhyme with each other, as in deep, sleep, keep, and weep, and the last word of lines designated "b" all rhyme with each other, as in day, away, stay, and gray. The last six lines rhymed in a variation of a *cdecde*, *cdccdc*, or *cdedce* pattern.

The Italian sonnet was introduced to England in the early part of the sixteenth century by English statesman and poet Thomas Wyatt (1503–1542). As it developed the English sonnet came to differ significantly from the Italian form. It was divided into four units: three quatrains (four-line parts), each with its own rhyme scheme, followed by a rhymed couplet, or two lines of rhymed verse. Thus the typical rhyme scheme for the English sonnet is: *ababcdcdefefgg*, but there are many variations. Philip Sidney was one of the developers of the English sonnet and popularized the sonnet sequence in England. In the sonnet below, he uses the English form, with three quatrains and a couplet, to express the conventional theme of unrequited love. Note the letters in parentheses at the end of each line, indicating this simple *ababababcdcdee* rhyme scheme.

Sonnet I from *Astrophil and Stella*

Loving in truth, and fain [intent] in verse
    my love to show, (a)
That she (dear She) might take some
    pleasure of my pain: (b)
Pleasure might cause her read, reading
    might make her know, (a)
Knowledge might pity win, and pity
    grace obtain; (b)
I sought fit words to paint the blackest
    face of woe, (a)
Studying inventions fine [other poets'
    creative works], her wits to
    entertain: (b)
Oft turning others' leaves [pages], to
    see if thence would flow (a)
Some fresh and fruitful showers upon
    my sun-burn'd brain. (b)
But words came halting forth, wanting
    Invention's stay, (c)
Invention, Nature's child, fled step-
    dame Study's blows, (d)
And others' feet still seem'd but
    strangers in my way. (c)
Thus, great with child to speak, and
    helpless in my throes [spasms;
    comparing poetry-writing to child-
    birth], (d)
Biting my truant [duty-shirking] pen,
    beating myself for spite (e)
"Fool," said my Muse [source of inspi-
    ration] to me, "look in thy heart and
    write." (e)

SOURCE OF POEM: *POET'S CORNER.*
HTTP://WWW.THEOTHERPAGES.ORG/
POEMS/INDEX.HTML.

passion for a married woman named Stella, expressing both the joy and anguish of being in love and the great divide between the sexual desires of the body and the moral reasoning of the mind. The sonnets are full of Petrarchan features, such as exaggerated comparisons and ornate imagery, but Sidney had developed a truly English form. The characters of his sequence speak in English accents and discuss national issues. Beyond this, Sidney's meter (the pattern of stressed and unstressed syllables), his rhyme scheme, and imagery are uniquely English. *Astrophil and Stella,* was not published until after his death in 1591. Upon its publication many English writers began to create sonnets. Sidney's poems and the works that followed, written by poets such as Edmund Spenser (c. 1552–1599), Fulke Greville (1554–1628), Michael Drayton (1563–1631), and William Shakespeare (1564–1616), represent the best of Elizabethan poetry.

Edmund Spenser and *The Faerie Queene*

Edmund Spenser was the son of a humble cloth maker who worked hard to get an education. When he was twenty-seven Spenser wrote *The Shepheardes Calender* (1579), a series of twelve short, descriptive poems that focused on the lives of shepherds, idealizing their pastoral, or country, life. The pastoral style of the work, which was popular in the Elizabethan Era, was drawn from the works of Roman poet Virgil (70–19 BCE). The poems are noted for their rustic language and their graceful rhythm. With this publication, Spenser became one of England's best-known poets.

A friend introduced Spenser to Robert Dudley, who used his influence at court to win Spenser a position as secretary to the Lord Deputy of Ireland. Settled in Ireland Spenser began writing his masterpiece, *The Faerie Queene.* He planned to write twelve books, each focusing on a moral virtue such as holiness, justice, or temperance. Each virtue was represented by a knight. Amidst the moral virtues, however, Spenser also wrote about political issues and religious themes. *The Faerie Queene* presents a complex religious, national, and philosophical allegory that describes the struggle between good and evil, presents the history of the ongoing battle between English Protestantism and Roman Catholicism, and expresses the views of the Anglican church. All the books of *The Faerie Queene* are connected by the presence of two characters, Prince Arthur, representing the legendary figure of King Arthur, and the Faerie

Queene, who represents Queen Elizabeth. The entire work is presented as a celebration of Elizabeth's reign and greatly flatters the queen.

The Faerie Queene follows the literary form of a romance. The book also took its form from the popular handbook of manners, a book that instructed Elizabethan gentlemen on the proper code of behavior. But Spenser aimed higher than either of these forms. *The Faerie Queene* was his attempt to create an English epic, a long narrative poem that relates the deeds of a hero and is of particular importance to a culture or nation.

By 1589 Spenser had finished the first three books of his projected twelve-book project. (He would finish only six volumes during his lifetime.) He brought them to London, where they were published early in the following year with an elaborate dedication to Elizabeth. While some English poets criticized *The Faerie Queene* because Spenser had used the rough, old-fashioned language of Chaucer, most scholars and general readers enjoyed the poem and marveled at Spenser's mastery of poetic skills. It was written with clarity and grace in an innovative rhyme scheme that gave it a slow and stately movement. The nine-line stanza Spenser invented for his epic has come to be known as the Spenserian stanza, and many poets after him have tried to imitate his rhythm. (A stanza is a group of lines that form a section of a poem.)

The queen, too, was highly impressed with the poem. Spenser hoped she would grant him a large pension to enable him to concentrate on his verse. But this was not to be. In an unwise move, Spenser sharply criticized her chief advisor, William Cecil (Lord Burghley; 1520–1598), in a 1591 publication. His criticism was not appreciated, and he would forever remain an outsider in the royal court. Early in 1591 he returned to Ireland and resumed work on his epic, publishing three more books in 1595. The poet died in 1599. His extensive poetic vocabulary, his natural ear for rhythm and rhyme, and his subtle introduction of political and social issues of the day into his works would change the way English poets wrote. Many scholars rank Spenser among the greatest poets of the English language.

Shakespeare, the poet

Around 1592 the plague (a deadly and highly contagious disease) forced the London theaters to close. At that time the young playwright William Shakespeare published his first long narrative poem called *Venus and Adonis*. The 1,194-line erotic (concerning sexual love and desire) and mythological poem was based on a version of the myth of Venus and

Adonis found in the *Metamorphoses* by the Roman poet Ovid (43–17 BCE), Shakespeare's favorite poet. Shakespeare's poem is a comical treatment of love, in which a goddess awkwardly tries to seduce an unresponsive young man. Shakespeare wrote the poem in the elaborate language popular at the time, not unlike the language of John Lyly's romances. A year later Shakespeare published *The Rape of Lucrece,* a more dramatic poem than the first. The story, derived from Ovid and other classical sources, relates the rape of a virtuous, married noblewoman, Lucrece, by the son of the king of Rome. Lucrece kills herself and her death brings about a full-scale revolt against the royal family, which in turn leads to the founding of the Roman Republic. Both of Shakespeare's early long poems carefully follow the form and structure of classical poetry. They were extremely popular and went through many printings, establishing Shakespeare's reputation as a major poet.

Historians believe that Shakespeare probably began his most famous poems, a sequence of 154 sonnets, not long after writing the two earlier poems, though they were not published until 1609. One hundred and twenty six of the sonnets are addressed to a young man of high rank for whom the poet has strong feelings of love. Most of the rest of the sonnets have to do with the poet's mistress, often called the "Dark Lady" by critics. The sonnets seem intimate and heartfelt, like expressions of the poet's own life. Many scholars have attempted to identify the young man and the dark lady from among the real people in Shakespeare's life, but there is no conclusive evidence to support their ideas. It is possible that the narrator is not actually Shakespeare's own voice, but an invented character.

Shakespeare arrived late to the English sonnet-writing trend, and he followed the contemporary conventions of form, adding a few new touches to the rhyme scheme. His major addition to the form was in each sonnet's last two rhyming lines—the couplet—which in many of Shakespeare's sonnets sounds like a philosophical summary in a voice more detached and assured than the rest of the sonnet.

It was the themes of Shakespeare's sonnets, however, that challenged the poetic conventions of the time. It was expected that a sonnet would be about a young man's worship of a beautiful young woman who does not return his love. But Shakespeare's sonnets address the worship of a young nobleman by an older poet. In the poems addressed to a woman the narrator declares that his mistress is not beautiful, virtuous, or even honest. Because Shakespeare veers so far away from the conventional themes, his readers cannot assume he is merely imitating the sentiments of other poets before him. Thus the sonnets take on a feeling of reality that was unparalleled in his time as they reflect on a variety of conventional and unconventional themes: the sorrow of growing older, unrequited love, and the inconstancies of human society. The narrator of the sonnets never looks to a god for help, but sometimes finds comfort in the act of writing poetry.

Shakespeare's sonnet series is considered a literary masterpiece. In his lifetime it established him as one of England's top poets. In later years most Elizabethan poetry, with the exception of Spenser's *The Faerie Queene,* lost its popular audience, but Shakespeare's sonnets are still widely read today. Scholars often place the sonnets on an equal level with Shakespeare's dramas as some of the greatest literature of all time.

For More Information

BOOKS

Brimacombe, Peter. *All the Queen's Men: The World of Elizabeth I.* New York: St. Martin's Press, 2000.

Greenblatt, Stephen. *Will in the World: How Shakespeare Became Shakespeare.* New York: W. W. Norton and Co., 2004.

Palliser, D. M. *The Age of Elizabeth: England Under the Later Tudors, 1547–1603,* 2d ed. London and New York: Longman, 1992.

WEB SITES

Best, Michael. "John Lyly and the Euphuistic Style." *Shakespeare's Life and Times.* Internet Shakespeare Editions, University of Victoria: Victoria, BC, 2001–2005. http://ise.uvic.ca/Library/SLT/intro/introcite.html (accessed on July 11, 2006).

"Elizabethan Sonneteers." *Sonnet Central.* http://www.sonnets.org/eliz.htm (accessed on July 11, 2006).

"Shakespeare's Sonnets." http://www.shakespeares-sonnets.com/ (accessed on July 11, 2006).

Sidney, Philip. "Astrophil and Stella." *Poet's Corner.* http://www.theotherpages.org/poems/index.html. (accessed on July 11, 2006).

Sidney, Philip. "The Defence of Poesie." *Renascence Editions, University of Oregon.* http://darkwing.uoregon.edu/~rbear/defence.html (accessed on July 11, 2006).

10

Elizabethan Drama

Of all the arts in Elizabethan England, drama was the most popular, and left behind the most enduring legacy. Not a single theater existed in England until well after Elizabeth I (1533–1603) took the throne in 1558. Within two decades of the building of the first major theater in the mid-1570s, however, a huge and varied body of Elizabethan comedy, tragedy, revenge plays, and history chronicles arose. Rising Elizabethan dramatists like John Lyly (1554–1606), Christopher Marlowe (1564–1593), and Thomas Kyd (1558–1594) surpassed the limits of known drama—European theater and the classical drama of ancient Greece and Rome—by portraying complex political, psychological, and historical themes. The most noted playwright of the English language, William Shakespeare (1564–1616), was only twelve years old when the first theater was built in England. With his plays Shakespeare brought Elizabethan drama—and English culture in general—to unexpected new heights.

At the beginning of the Elizabethan Era, the period associated with the reign of Queen Elizabeth I (1558–1603) that is often considered to be a golden age in English history, most English drama was based on two ancient genres: mystery plays and morality plays. Mystery plays were simple enactments of scenes from the Bible. Performed in churches or churchyards, they were popular on religious holidays like Christmas and Easter. Morality plays were allegories (stories that represent abstract ideas or principles as characters, figures, or events) that depicted a struggle between the forces of good and evil. The characters of these plays had names like Justice or Vice. They did not have developed personalities because they were intended to represent either a moral virtue or a form of evil rather than a flesh-and-blood human being. Morality plays could be very long—some lasted an entire day—and their goal was to improve their audiences' moral behavior.

By the mid-sixteenth century new variations on morality plays had arisen, reflecting the audiences' growing desire to be entertained.

WORDS TO KNOW

allegory: A story or painting that represents abstract ideas or principles as characters, figures, or events.

amphitheater: A large, semi-circular outdoor theater with seats rising in tiers from a central acting area.

blank verse: A type of poetry with regular meter (the pattern of stressed and unstressed syllables) but no rhyme.

capitalism: An economic system in which private individuals or companies own and invest in the country's businesses and industries with little government control.

comedy: Plays written in a light and amusing manner that present the struggles and eventual successes of everyday heroes as they overcome non-life-threatening problems.

farce: Comedy that presents absurd characters and scenes in order to make the audience laugh.

heresy: A religious opinion that conflicts with the church's doctrines.

history chronicle: A play based on historic people or events.

iambic foot: A unit of poetic meter that consists of one unstressed syllable followed by one stressed syllable, as in the sound of da-DUM.

iambic pentameter: A poetic line that contains five iambic units.

idolatry: The worship of religious icons (sacred images, statues, objects, and monuments).

mystery play: A play enacting a scene or scenes from the Bible.

pageant: A dramatic presentation, such as a play, that often depicts a historical, biblical, or traditional event.

Puritans: A group of Protestants who follow strict religious standards.

Reformation: A sixteenth-century religious movement that aimed to reform the Roman Catholic Church and resulted in the establishment of Protestant churches.

revenge tragedy: A play concerned the theme of vengeance for a past wrong—usually murder.

romance: A literary work about improbable events involving characters that are quite different from ordinary people.

soliloquy: A speech in which a character, alone on stage, expresses his or her thoughts aloud.

tragedy: Drama of a serious nature, usually featuring an admirable but flawed hero who undergoes a serious struggle ending in a devastating downfall.

Playwrights wanted to amuse their audiences rather than preach to them. They added farce (comedy that presents absurd characters and scenes in order to make the audience laugh) or current political events, thinly disguised in order to avoid trouble with the authorities. Some plays incorporated the local events of the village in which they were being performed, presenting hastily written plots about the latest scandal or catastrophe. This timely, relevant subject matter appealed to the villagers. Often the characters representing vice or evil were given the largest roles so that they could create more chaos on stage in the spirit of fun. The plays in the early years of Elizabeth's reign blended different types of drama: morality play, farce, English history play, and pastoral drama, which idealized country settings. The plays were often secular (non-religious) and much shorter than the morality plays of the past. They were rarely written down, however, so today we know about them only from descriptions in letters and journals from the time.

Early acting companies

By the 1550s plays were almost exclusively being performed by acting companies—small groups of four to ten adult men and possibly a boy or two. Women were not permitted to act on stage until long after the Elizabethan Era, so female parts were played by boys or men dressed as women. The acting companies traveled from town to town carrying their stage scenery and costumes in wagons. Although most townspeople were eager to be entertained, the local authorities and religious leaders viewed the acting companies as a threat to the morals, health, and safety of their towns. At the time actors were not viewed as working artists; they were usually scorned for being homeless and unemployed. Indeed, though some acting troops were honest professionals, others were notorious for committing petty crimes and behaving improperly.

In 1572 Elizabeth banned all companies that were not bound to a patron, a nobleman who was responsible for them. This law made it difficult for the troublemakers to stay in business, since no one would sponsor them. All troops soon became known by their patron's name. Some of the major acting companies in the early 1570s were Leicester's Men, the company that worked for Robert Dudley (Earl of Leicester; 1532–1588), Lord Oxford's Men, Lord Admiral's Men, Lord Buckingham's Men, and so forth. On special occasions these acting companies performed at their patron's estates to entertain guests. But the noble patrons did not financially support the acting troops, and to earn a living the companies spent most of their time traveling throughout England, performing for any town that agreed to let them set up their makeshift stage in the yard of a local inn. Local farmers and working people, as well as the upper classes, eagerly gathered to watch, paying what they could when a hat was passed around to collect money after the performance.

A traveling acting company performs a play in the yard of a London inn. THE GRANGER COLLECTION, LTD.

Regulating the plays

The Reformation—the sixteenth-century religious movement that aimed to reform the Roman Catholic Church and resulted in the establishment of Protestant churches—created an altogether new environment for drama. During the reign of the Catholic Mary I (1516–1558; reigned 1553–58), mystery and morality plays had been popular, and the Bible was viewed as the most appropriate source for drama. When Elizabeth took the throne and made Anglicanism (a form of Protestantism) the national religion, she was concerned that religious plays would be used to stir English Catholics against the Anglican church and herself. In 1559 Elizabeth prohibited all plays that were not licensed by the crown. Drama quickly became more secular. In accordance with Protestant beliefs, in the 1570s she banned all mystery plays in which men played the role of God, which were considered by Protestants to be idolatry, or the worship of religious icons (sacred

A Taste for Violence

The English population in the mid-sixteenth century had a large appetite for blood and gore in their entertainment. They did not consider the theater as high art, but rather as a spectator entertainment along the lines of bearbaiting and cockfighting.

In a bearbaiting a bear was tied to a stake in the middle of a ring, and bound with tethers that allowed the bear to reach only a short distance. The stagers of the bearbaiting set packs of large dogs loose to viciously attack the bear. Despite the tethers, the bear often killed or disabled dogs that were not quick enough to escape its deadly claws. Faster dogs, though, brutally tore up the bear. The bears were used over and over and became well known to the crowds, who cheered them on by name. Sometimes the dogs would kill the bear as the crowds breathlessly watched.

In cockfighting the owners of roosters tied sharp blades to the birds' feet and then placed them in a pit to fight. The birds would continue to mutilate each other with their blades until one of them died. The spectators usually bet large sums on their favorite bird.

Bearbaiting and cockfighting were extremely popular among most of the English people, including the rich and the poor, the educated and the illiterate. Queen Elizabeth enjoyed watching bearbaiting, and she ordered it performed for visiting diplomats from Europe as a special treat. Bearbaiting pits were situated close to the early theaters. It was not unusual for a family to divide their holiday afternoon between watching a bearbaiting and attending a play. To compete, the plays often provided violent action such as sword fights, murder, and other bloody crimes onstage.

images, statues, objects, and monuments). Many other religious plays were banned, particularly those that allowed too much freedom of the imagination in dealing with Bible stories, which many Protestants believed should be understood literally, that is, according to the exact words of the Bible. The effect of this regulation was to shift the dramatic arts away from religion.

In 1574 Elizabeth placed her Master of the Revels in charge of licensing all plays performed in England. The Master of the Revels was an officer of the state who worked for the Lord Chamberlain, the chief officer of the royal household. The queen's Master of Revels had the authority to censor all English plays. He could ban entire plays or delete parts of plays that were considered objectionable, and it was his job to eliminate anything that seemed to be critical of the queen or the Anglican church. For a time the crown licensed only a few acting troops, but the demand for plays in London was so great that competing acting companies arose and prospered despite the regulations.

London and the first theaters

By late sixteenth century London was a bustling city of about two hundred thousand people. The city had become the center of a thriving capitalist economy. (Capitalism is an economic system in which private individuals or companies own and invest in the country's businesses and industries with little government control.) There was a large demand for entertainment among all segments of London's population—working people, merchants, and nobles. Intelligent investors quickly learned there was money to be made in the theater.

In 1576 actor James Burbage (1531–1597) decided to build a permanent structure in which plays could be staged. He called it simply The Theater. The Theater was a huge amphitheater (a large semi-circular outdoor theater with seats rising in tiers from a central acting area), capable of holding about three thousand spectators. It had a very large outdoor stage with a small, enclosed room at the back, in which the actors changed costumes and waited for their cues to go on stage. The stage was surrounded on all sides by a yard into which standing spectators crowded for the low admission of one penny. These crowds ate, drank, talked, and moved around in the standing yard as the play was performed. It was necessary for the acting to be extremely bold and loud to compete with the commotion in the yard. For those who could afford higher priced tickets, there were three tiers of seating along the walls above the standing yard. For the wealthy, there were enclosed boxes over the stage.

Playhouses were not allowed within the city because authorities viewed the theaters as a cause of lawlessness, neglect of work, and the spread of the plague, a deadly and highly contagious disease. London's city leaders were mostly Puritans (a group of Protestants that followed strict religious standards), and believed that acting in itself was ungodly. Puritans considered it a sin to play any role other than one's own God-given identity. But even with the flood of Puritan sermons and pamphlets against the theater, the London public could not get enough of it. Because of the city's restrictions, investors simply built theaters outside of city limits but within walking distance.

The Theater did so well that five more amphitheater playhouses were built in areas surrounding London: the Curtain in 1577, the Rose in 1587, the Swan in 1595, the Globe in 1599, and the Fortune in 1600. The Swan, Rose, and Globe were all built across the Thames River in the Bankside district. The amphitheater playhouse neighborhoods, much to the concern of the Puritans, were filled with taverns, gambling dens, and

A model of the Globe Theater. © ADAM WOOLFITT/CORBIS.

houses of prostitution, as well as bearbaiting and cockfighting pits. The neighborhoods became notorious for petty crimes such as picking pockets and fist fighting, but crowds continued to fill the theaters anyway.

Theater for the upper classes only

The large amphitheaters outside the city attracted people of all classes, but these were not the only places where dramas were performed. The most prestigious site for drama was the royal court. Elizabeth was extremely fond of theater. Initially her favorite nobles tried to amuse her by presenting their own plays, but as the London theater improved the queen preferred the professionals. In 1583 Elizabeth instructed her Master of the Revels to bring together a company of the top actors in England. Leading actors were selected from all the good acting companies and these became the Lord Chamberlain's Men. For actors nothing promised a brighter or more lucrative future than being selected to play in the royal court.

Elite audiences might also attend plays in the halls of schools, universities, and law courts. Young boys at the Chapel Royal and St. Paul's Cathedral choir schools in London began to perform plays around 1575. Higher admission was charged at these smaller and more intimate indoor halls than at the amphitheaters. The audiences tended to be educated and wealthy, and the plays were more likely to be based on the Greek and Roman classics, using highly elaborate language. Some were even performed in Latin. Because of regulations against public playhouses within the city of London, private theaters were built on former monastery and church grounds that were not under the control of the city authorities.

The acting companies

In 1578 the queen, trying to keep the theater under control, licensed only six acting companies: the Children of the Chapel Royal, the Children of St. Paul's, the Lord Chamberlain's Men, Lord Warwick's Men, Leicester's Men, and Essex's Men. These companies, and others that arose later, became competitive businesses. Most companies had been formed by a core group of actors who had invested in them. These investors were called sharers, or partners, and they divided up the profits of the company among themselves. Though the sharers were often the principal actors in the company, they hired other actors as well. Hoping to compete with other companies, the sharers hired writers to create entertaining and popular plays and searched for top-quality actors. Every actor in the company had a specialty: some played clowns, some played warriors, and some played women. All actors were expected to be able to sing, dance, and do their own stunts in battle scenes. By the 1580s the acting companies that had survived the competition had become highly professional.

Playwrights: The University Wits

For centuries the purpose of England's two large universities, Cambridge and Oxford, had been to educate young men who were preparing for the clergy. By the 1570s, though, increasing numbers of middle-class young men were attending college, far too many for all of them to enter careers in the church. The growing theater industry presented a new opportunity for some of the recent university graduates. By the late sixteenth century the theater companies produced new plays on an almost daily basis; by one estimate, at least fifteen hundred plays were produced during the Elizabethan Era. Theater companies sought writers who could quickly write entertaining plays. Becoming a professional playwright was suddenly an acceptable way for educated young men to earn a living. It is important to note, however, that university-educated young gentlemen would never consider acting in a theater company or participating in the business aspect of the company, as this was considered beneath their social standing.

A small group of top professional playwrights, known as the University Wits, arose from 1584 to 1594. These young men developed the signature characteristics of Elizabethan drama. Included in this group were: John Lyly, George Peele (c. 1556–1596), Robert Greene (1558–1592), Thomas Kyd, and Christopher Marlowe. Lyly had made a name for himself with his prose fiction (see Chapter 9). In the 1580s he became an assistant director of the child acting company of St. Paul's Cathedral. He also worked for the Queen's Men, and he wrote plays for both companies. In his early dramas Lyly used his highly elaborate style, but in his later works he began to experiment with the more natural manner of ancient Roman comedy. (A comedy is a play written in a light and amusing manner that presents the struggles and eventual successes of everyday heroes as they overcome ordinary problems.) Though Lyly is considered only a minor playwright today, he was nevertheless a pioneer in the development of the romantic comedy and a strong influence on the playwrights who followed him.

George Peele brought a different set of standards to English theater. He had a strong interest in pageantry, derived from his father's work as a designer of pageants, or dramatic presentations that often depict a historical, biblical, or traditional event. His plays, often written for church events, can be seen as attempts to match spectacle and poetry to dramatic action, and he was known for both history chronicles (plays based on historic people or events) and biblical plays.

Robert Greene's best-known plays, *The Honourable History of Friar Bacon and Friar Bungay* and *The Scottish History of James the Fourth,* are a blend of humor, myth, history, and fairy-tale. They are notable for creating a strong sense of the specific world in which the play takes place. This world, though fanciful and idealized, is recognizably Elizabethan.

Thomas Kyd

Thomas Kyd produced his most significant (and only surviving) work, *The Spanish Tragedy,* sometime between 1583 and 1589. This extremely

Title Page of The Spanish
Tragedy *by Thomas Kyd.*

popular play did much to shape the great tragedies to come. Tragedy is serious drama, usually featuring an admirable but flawed hero who undergoes a momentous struggle that ends in a devastating downfall. Tragedy had developed in ancient Greece and Rome, but had not yet found popularity in Europe. Kyd found his model for the *The Spanish*

Tragedy in the tragedies of the ancient Roman playwright Seneca (c. 4 BCE –65 CE), whose bloody chronicles of royal family history were well known among Elizabethans. In Kyd's play a father, driven mad by grief over his son's murder, plans revenge. He stages a play in which the murderers are enlisted as actors. In a sword-fight scene in this play-within-the-play the murderers are actually stabbed to death before an unsuspecting audience's eyes. The father then relates to the audience the story of his son's murder. He then bites out his own tongue before killing himself. Kyd's play was the first Elizabethan example of a popular genre that became known as the revenge tragedy, a play concerned with the theme of vengeance for a past wrong—usually murder. *Hamlet,* Shakespeare's famous (and only) revenge play, is thought to be taken from a play Kyd wrote known as *Ur-Hamlet* (or "original Hamlet") that has not survived.

The Spanish Tragedy is viewed as a crude example of Elizabethan tragedy today. Its speeches are very artificial and its gory violence is similar to today's bloody horror films. But it was immensely popular in its own time. It gave the English audience the gore it demanded, and at the same time presented the downfall of hated enemies, the Spanish, with whom the English were at war at the time. Kyd's play glorifies England as God's chosen place on Earth.

Christopher Marlowe

Christopher Marlowe was the son of a shoemaker who, with the help of a scholarship, obtained his master's degree at Cambridge in 1587. Marlowe associated with some influential members of the court, such as explorer and statesman Walter Raleigh (1552–1618) and poet Edmund Spenser (c. 1552–1599), and he was closely acquainted with the queen's secretary of state, Francis Walsingham (1532–1590). Many historians believe that Marlowe was one of Walsingham's spies, working undercover to expose Catholic plots against the queen, but this has not been proved. In his short life of twenty-nine years, Marlowe became known for his wild, nonconforming ways. He was an avowed atheist, or someone who does not believe in God, and he was said to have openly promoted homosexuality. At a young age he was involved in killing a man, though this was eventually determined an act of self defense.

The six or seven plays Marlowe managed to write before his early death were highly successful. In 1587 his play *Tamburlaine* was first staged in one of the London theaters. Its hero, Tamburlaine, is a shepherd who forms a gang of warriors. He stops at nothing to fulfill his ambition for power. Tamburlaine becomes a mighty conqueror of several kingdoms. Even after his successful advancement from peasant to ruler, he continues to conquer distant territories. Tamburlaine declares that, though he was born a peasant, he was meant to rule. His success in conquering monarchs who inherited their power by a claim of divine right calls into question the very basis of the English power system. In Elizabeth's time it was considered treason to question the divine right of the monarch. Nonetheless, this bloody and violent play was extremely popular with English audiences. After the first part of *Tamburlaine* met with great success, a sequel followed.

Tamburlaine is remembered not only for its drama, but also for being the first English tragedy to successfully use blank verse. Blank verse is a type of poetry with regular meter (the pattern of stressed and unstressed syllables) but no rhyme. In English the meter most commonly used in blank verse was iambic pentameter, a poetic line that contains five iambic units called feet. An iambic foot consists of one unstressed syllable followed by a stressed syllable, as in the sound of da-DUM. In the following lines of blank verse from *Tamburlaine, Part One,* Act IV, Scene ii, the stressed syllable of the iambic unit is in bold:

> His **spear**, his **shield**, his **horse**, his **arm** our **plumes**,
> And **jet**ty **feath**ers, **men** ace **death** and **hell**;
> With**out** res**pect** of **sex**, de**gree** or **age**,
> He **raz**eth **all** his **foes** with **fire** and **sword**.

The repetitive sounds of the iambic units created a chant-like sound that elevated the language above the sound of everyday speech and was thus appropriate for the solemn tone of tragedy. Marlowe varied the rhythm when he wanted to bring the tone down to a more humble or uncertain level. Blank verse had been used before in English poetry, but Marlowe so greatly improved it that it came to be known as "Marlowe's mighty line." Well into the next century blank verse was the dominant form for English tragedy.

Marlowe went on to write several other notable plays, including *The Jew of Malta,* after which Shakespeare modeled his *The Merchant of Venice. Doctor Faustus,* generally considered Marlowe's greatest work, was probably also his last. Its central figure, a scholar who feels he already knows everything available to human learning, attempts to gain the ultimate knowledge and power by selling his soul to the devil. The high point of the play comes in the portrayal of the hero's final moments, as he awaits the powers of darkness that demand his soul.

Although earlier English dramatists had achieved success in the field of comedy, Marlowe and Kyd made the first significant advances in tragedy. Unlike Kyd's rather crude dramatic lines, however, Marlowe's blank verse proved remarkably effective. Marlowe's poetic line and his drama earned him the title of the greatest dramatist in England—until the almost immediate rise of Shakespeare.

Shakespeare

William Shakespeare was born six years after Elizabeth took the throne, in the prosperous market town of Stratford-upon-Avon. Little is known about Shakepeare's early life, but by 1592 he had apparently begun building a reputation in the London theater. Around this time Shakespeare wrote some of his early plays, such as his first tragedy *Titus Andronicus*; the comedies *The Two Gentlemen of Verona, The Taming of the Shrew,* and *Love's Labour's Lost*; and the history series, *Henry VI (Parts 1 and 2)* and *Richard III.* The plays were not published; he wrote a handwritten working draft for the actors.

In 1594 Shakespeare became the principal writer for the Lord Chamberlain's Men. The Lord Chamberlain's Men became the foremost London acting company, performing at Elizabeth's court on thirty-two occasions between 1594 and 1603, whereas their chief rivals, the Lord Admiral's Men, made only twenty appearances at court during these years. Most historians attribute the success of the Lord Chamberlain's Men to the fact that, after joining the group in 1594, Shakespeare wrote for no other company.

Shakespeare produced a steady assortment of plays between 1589 and 1613. Like most playwrights of his time, he rarely wrote original story lines. He took his plots and characters from ancient Greek and Roman stories, modern European plays, folklore, and history. Shakespeare wrote in four dramatic categories: comedy, history, tragedy, and romance, or literary works about improbable events involving characters that are quite different from ordinary people. Yet for Shakespeare the lines between these categories were not firm. There is comedy mixed in with his tragedy and often a dark side to his comedies. Some of his histories are considered tragedies, while the romances are often grouped with the comedies. His plays are known for their side plots that are

William Shakespeare at work.

sometimes more interesting than the main plots. In addition, his plays appeal to people from all walks of life, from peasants to nobles.

Comedies

Shakespeare's comedies of the period 1596–1602 included *A Midsummer Night's Dream, The Merchant of Venice, As You Like It,* and *Twelfth Night.* These plays focus on themes of courtship and marriage. Though most of the romantic comedies are taken from Italian sources, Shakespeare introduced his own inventions to the plots. They almost always hinge on a case of mistaken identity or some other type of mistake. Some of these mistakes are caused when a female character takes on a male identity.

Another feature of Shakespeare's comedies are the imaginary realms, such as the forest of *A Midsummer Night's Dream,* that provide an escape from the restrictions of society, particularly the law and the social hierarchy. In the relative freedom of such places, conflicts are resolved, permitting a happy ending that typically involves marriage and a renewed society. The comedies have been some of Shakespeare's most popular plays throughout the centuries. Shakespeare's dark comedies, including *Troilus and Cressida, All's Well That Ends Well,* and *Measure for Measure,* are characterized by much more serious themes and dark tones.

History plays

Shakespeare's history plays reflect his reliance on two principal sources: Edward Hall's *The Union of the Two Noble and Illustre Families of Lancastre and York* (1548) and Raphael Holinshed's *Chronicles of England, Scotlande, and Irlande* (1587). Both works promote the belief that an act of divine (God's) will unified England under Tudor rule, starting with Elizabeth's grandfather, Henry VII, in 1485 and ending with her death in 1603. Eight of Shakespeare's ten history plays collectively trace the period of English monarchy from the fourteenth century to the emergence of the Tudors. They are commonly grouped in two sets: the first contains the three parts of *Henry VI* and *Richard III*; the second, depicting chronologically earlier events but written later in Shakespeare's career, includes *Richard II,* the two parts of *Henry IV,* and *Henry V.*

The second history series is considered the most successful. The series begins in *Richard II* when the forceful nobleman Bolingbroke deposes the weak King Richard II. It continues through the two parts of Henry IV, in which the wonderfully amoral and fat knight Falstaff accompanies the rebellious Prince Hal, Bolingbroke's son, in a series of petty crimes and unprincely antics. In *Henry V* Hal blossoms into England's honest and valiant king and leads a newly unified England to triumph in a battle with France. The audience feels satisfied with the heroic king in the end, but at the same time many feel deprived of Falstaff who, though dishonest and amoral, was the source of human bonding and joy in the earlier plays. The character Falstaff is acclaimed as one of Shakespeare's most imaginative comic characterizations. English legend has it that Elizabeth liked

Falstaff so well in the history series she asked Shakespeare to write another play featuring him, and the result was *The Merry Wives of Windsor.*

Though the second history series seems to support the divine right of the Tudors to reign over England, according to some critics the plays have the opposite effect, subtly exposing the defects of divine-right monarchy. Elizabeth herself was aware of this. In 1601 statesman Robert Devereux (Earl of Essex; 1566–1601), staged an ill-fated uprising against the queen. Some of Essex's followers arranged a performance of *Richard II* in the hope that Shakespeare's depiction of the removal of an unfit monarch would generate support for their cause. Elizabeth, upon hearing of the performance, angrily cried, as quoted by Stephen Greenblatt in *Will in the World: How Shakespeare Became Shakespeare*: "I am Richard II. Know ye not that?"

Tragedies

Shakespeare's tragedies differ greatly from one another, but many share a few notable features. Usually the protagonist's best and most heroic traits are what destroy him. Even in the darkest tragedy there is a mix of comic and tragic characters. Politics are ever-present in Shakespeare's tragedies, and though the events are always presented in a different time or setting (to avoid censorship or even criminal charges), many of the tragedies' political themes are recognizably Elizabethan.

Critics have labeled four of Shakespeare's tragedies as the great tragedies: *Hamlet, King Lear, Macbeth,* and *Othello.* Special mention should be made of Shakespeare's much earlier tragedy, *Romeo and Juliet,* which remains one of the most frequently performed Shakespearean dramas. The great tragedies were written during Shakespeare's last decade as a playwright. As he got older Shakespeare seems to have become less willing to depict humans as all good or all bad. His heroes of the later tragedies are dominated by passions that are not strictly noble. What destroys the hero is what is best about him, yet the best qualities in Macbeth, a power-hungry king-killer, or Othello, who is lost to his obsessive sexual jealousy, are not as sympathetic as Romeo's overwhelming love for Juliet. In these later tragedies Shakespeare depicts a world in disorder, in which evil is as likely to dominate as goodness.

Romances

A final group of plays are called the romances. *Cymbeline, The Winter's Tale,* and *The Tempest* share their conventions with the tragicomedy, a popular form of Elizabethan play that fell into both the tragedy and comedy categories. Like his comedies Shakespeare's romances end on a happy note, but they are solemn in tone and they focus more on the human community as a whole than on the individual characters of the play. Romance characters, like those of the old morality plays, tend to represent an aspect of human life rather than embodying complex personalities like Shakespeare's other characters. Resolution of the romance is often reached through supernatural forces that the characters do not understand.

Shakespeare lived his life without leaving much trace of who he was or what he was like, but so did many other writers of his time. But thanks to two of his actors, who published Shakespeare's plays in the *First Folio*, his plays have not been lost to history. Despite this mystery surrounding his life, Shakespeare's plays are the supreme example of the golden era of the arts in Elizabethan times. They are considered so important, in fact, that the Elizabethan period is frequently called the age of Shakespeare.

For More Information

BOOKS

Greenblatt, Stephen. *Will in the World: How Shakespeare Became Shakespeare.* New York: W. W. Norton, 2004.

Honan, Park. *Shakespeare: A Life.* Oxford, UK: Oxford University Press, 1998.

Picard, Liza. *Elizabeth's London: Everyday Life in Elizabethan London.* New York: St. Martin's Press, 2003.

Rowse, A. L. *What Shakespeare Read—And Thought.* New York: Coward, McCann and Geghegan, 1981.

Sams, Eric. *The Real Shakespeare: Retrieving the Early Years, 1564–1594.* New Haven and London: Yale University Press, 1995.

WEB SITES

Gray, Terry A. "Mr. William Shakespeare and the Internet." http://shakespeare.palomar.edu/ (accessed July 11, 2006).

Thorndike, Ashley. "Minor Elizabethan Drama." *The E-server Drama Collection.* http://drama.eserver.org/criticism/minor_elizabethan_drama.html (accessed July 11, 2006).

11

Daily Life in the Elizabethan Era

Historians studying the Elizabethan Era, the period associated with the reign of Queen Elizabeth I (1558–1603) that is often considered to be a golden age in English history, have focused mainly on the lives of the era's wealthy nobles. (Nobles were the elite men and women who held social titles.) The nobles held great power and frequently lived colorful and extravagant lives, but they made up only about 3 percent of the population. Although the vast majority of the Elizabethan population was quite poor, few firsthand historical records of their daily lives have survived. Members of the lower classes in England were mainly uneducated, so they did not usually keep journals or written records describing their own lives. They could not afford to have their portraits painted nor to preserve their humble homes for future generations. Historians agree, though, that daily life for the majority of Elizabethans had little to do with courtly life, and much to do with working hard to earn a meager living.

From a feudal to commercial economy

The working classes of England had always had a difficult life. Under the feudal system of the Middle Ages (the period in European history lasting from c. 500 to c. 1500), powerful lords owned and governed local districts, which were usually made up of peasant families and ranged from fifty to a few hundred people. (Peasants were farmers who worked in the fields owned by wealthy lords.) About 95 percent of the population of England lived in these rural districts. The peasant farmers performed almost all of the labor. They farmed the land: about one-third of the land solely for the lord; a portion to support the local church; and the rest for their own use. Their daily lives were regulated by the seasons, and they tended to work from sunup to sundown, rarely traveling beyond their own village. The sick and elderly relied on the kindness of the lord for

WORDS TO KNOW

feudal system: The political and economic system of the Middle Ages, in which powerful lords owned and governed local districts and the people of their districts served their lords under bonds of loyalty.

literacy: Ability to read and write.

mortality rate: The frequency of deaths in proportion to a specific population.

nobles: Elite men and women who held social titles.

parish: The community served by one local church.

peasant: A class of farmers who worked in the fields owned by wealthy lords. Part of the crop was paid to the lord as rent.

poorhouse: A building maintained by parish funding to house the local needy.

Reformation: A sixteenth-century religious movement that aimed to reform the Roman Catholic Church and resulted in the establishment of Protestant churches.

saint: A deceased person who, due to his or her exceptionally good behavior during life, receives the official blessing of the church and is believed to be capable of interceding with God to protect people on earth.

sumptuary laws: Statutes regulating how extravagantly people of the various social classes could dress.

tilting: A military exercise performed for the queen, in which young nobles on horseback armed with lances (long spears) charged at one another in an attempt to throw their opponent from his horse. Also known as jousting.

vagrant: A person who wanders from town to town without a home or steady employment.

---

survival. Peasant life was usually fairly stable, but there was almost no chance of escaping the grinding toil from one generation to the next.

England's farming economy was forever changed by the outbreak of a terrible plague, or infectious disease, that arrived on the European continent in 1348, killing more than one-fourth of the population in a few years. Continued outbreaks of the plague are estimated to have killed from one-third to one-half of Europe's population by 1400. So many people died that many villages were left without lords, fields were left without farmers, and children were left without parents. With so many laborers dead, lords no longer had an easy supply of labor to farm their lands. By the early sixteenth century laborers found they could demand more money and better working conditions. For the first time it became possible for some enterprising peasants to take over the lands made vacant by the plague and become landowners themselves.

Another economic change took place in the early sixteenth century. England had developed a huge and highly profitable cloth-making industry. At first the industry relied on imported material to make cloth, but by the sixteenth century English landowners discovered that there was more profit to be made raising sheep for wool than in planting crops. Many peasants lost their livelihoods when the lands they had farmed were fenced off for sheep. They moved to the cities, which were prospering because of the new cloth industry and the other growing trades. However, the new industries provided few jobs for unskilled laborers. The peasants who were lucky enough to find work in the cities earned extremely low wages that barely fed them, and many of them were unable to find employment at all.

The rise of cities and towns

When Elizabeth I (1533–1603) became queen there were about 2.8 million people in England. The population rose significantly during her reign, to about 4.1 million. Many people lived in the countryside, but in the sixteenth century the town population grew at a greater rate. Prior to Elizabethan times, only about 5 percent of the population lived in cities and towns, but during her reign, about 15 percent of the rapidly growing population had become urban. As businesses and industries developed, a new middle class consisting of successful merchants and craftsman arose. These businesspeople thrived in the cities and often served in the urban government. During Elizabeth's reign, as never before, it was possible for city merchants to become extremely wealthy and rise in social status.

England's capital and largest city, London, underwent remarkable changes, growing to about two hundred thousand people during Elizabeth's reign. (The next largest English city, by comparison, was only about fifteen thousand people.) London's population was divided. It included a small but powerful population of wealthy nobles, a prospering middle class, and a large and impoverished lower class living in miserable conditions. In the filthy, crowded neighborhoods of the poor, raw sewage (waste matter) ran through the streets. Disease and crime were widespread. Laborers who came to London from the country frequently failed to find jobs. Homeless, they wandered in search of a way to feed themselves. Many turned to small crime, such as begging, picking pockets, and prostitution, simply to avoid starvation. There was little help for the sick, elderly, and orphans. The life expectancy, or average life span, of an Elizabethan was only 42 years, but it was much lower among the urban poor. English people of all classes feared the arrival of gangs of beggars and drifters in their towns and villages, bringing crime and immoral behavior into an otherwise hardworking and orderly society.

Elizabethan poor laws

Parliament, the English legislative body, passed several poor laws during Elizabeth's reign. The poor laws assigned the responsibility for maintaining the poor to the local church districts, or parishes (England was divided into fifteen thousand parishes). Local officials assessed how much money was needed to support their district's poor and then collected these funds from property owners. Elizabethan poor laws distinguished between the "deserving poor," such as the sick, elderly, and orphans, and the "undeserving poor"—those who were capable of working but chose not to. The undeserving poor were to be punished, while the deserving poor would receive some kind of local support in the form of food, money, clothing, or a stay at the local orphanage or poorhouse, a building maintained by parish funding to house the needy.

To enforce the poor laws, each community needed to be able to keep track of its own poor. Thus, the new laws required that every English citizen have a place that was legally designated as their home. It was nearly impossible for anyone without proof of a permanent job or lots of money to establish a new place of residence. There was little tolerance for vagrants, people who wander from town to town without a home or steady employment. Vagrants were taken into custody, punished with a public whipping, and then returned to their home village.

Elizabethan education

An extensive educational system developed in England during Elizabeth's reign, and the rate of literacy, or the ability of individuals to read and write, rose considerably. Only about one-fifth of the population could sign their own names at the beginning of the era, but by Elizabeth's death about one-third of the population was literate.

Education was by no means available to everyone, nor were all schools equal in quality. The children of nobility continued to receive their education in their homes from some of England's top scholars, who were hired at considerable expense as tutors. For the sons of the growing middle classes, though, there was an increasing opportunity for education in the country's public schools. (Girls were usually educated at home in the arts of homemaking.) Public schools were not free. The term "public" referred to the fact that the student went out into the world for his

Learning the ABCs

Elizabethan petty school students were usually given hornbooks to help them learn their letters. These simple textbooks consisted of a piece of paper containing text that was covered with a thin, transparent (see-through) sheet made from an animal's horn to protect the paper from wear and tear. The horn-covered page was then mounted on a square piece of wood with a handle. On the page was the alphabet written out in lower case and capital letters, the Lord's Prayer, and a few simple words. With this hornbook the children learned to read and write in English.

The English alphabet in Elizabeth's time did not look quite the same as it does today. It was made up of only twenty-four letters, unlike the modern twenty-six-letter alphabet. The "i" and "j" were the same letter, with the "j" being used as the capital letter at the beginning of the word and the "i" being used as a lower case letter in the middle of the word. Similarly, the "u" and "v" were the same letter, with the "v" used as the capital. Today there is no letter for the "th" sound, but in Elizabethan times this was represented by a letter that looks like our "y." Thus the word "ye" was pronounced "the."

education rather than being schooled at home. Poor children usually began working at very young ages and had neither the time to receive an education nor the money to pay for it.

Education was more widespread in the cities, where the middle classes were larger. Even some working-class parents in the cities were successful enough to be able to spare their sons from working full-time, and a growing number of working-class boys went to school for at least a couple of years—long enough to learn the basics of reading and writing in the English language.

Petty and grammar schools

Boys—and a few girls—from the ages of about five to seven attended petty schools. A petty school was run by an educated local woman, usually the wife of a town noble, in her own home. The children in petty school were taught to read and write English. They also received instruction about being good Christians, as well as other lessons in proper behavior, including such practical matters as table manners. The schools were rigorous, beginning at 6:00 or 7:00 AM and continuing until sundown. Beatings were commonly used to motivate the children to learn. Petty schools prepared their students for grammar schools.

Children attended grammar schools from the ages of seven to fourteen. In these schools children were taught to read and write in

Latin. Literacy in Latin prepared them to continue their educations at the university level, where all schoolwork was done in the Latin language. In grammar schools the works of the notable classical Latin playwrights and historians were used only for the purpose of teaching Latin grammar. Subjects like science and music were not taught, and only a small amount of arithmetic was presented.

At the age of fourteen upper- and middle-class boys who could afford to continue their education entered a university. During Elizabeth's time, universities educated more middle-class boys than ever before, and even some sons of very humble craftsmen were able to attend the universities on scholarships. Students at the universities studied in several areas: liberal arts, which included grammar, logic (the science that deals with the principles of reasoning), music, astronomy (the scientific study of the stars, planets, and other celestial bodies), and arithmetic; the arts, consisting of philosophy, rhetoric (the study of expressing one's self elegantly in writing and in the spoken word), and poetry; natural history (the study of nature); religion; medicine; and law.

Clothing

The Elizabethan Era is known for the elaborate outfits that men and women wore to court and elite social functions. Extremely detailed portraits of the wealthy have given us a clear idea of how they dressed. The wealthy wore furs and jewels, and the cloth of their garments featured extravagant embroidery. But theirs was not the typical fashion of the times. The poor and even the middle classes dressed more simply. However, few detailed portraits or records of the clothing of the poor remain.

In Elizabethan England one's clothing provided an observer with instant knowledge of one's social status. With a growing middle class, the rich and powerful clung to their age-old distinction of wearing clothes that made it immediately clear that they outranked others. Sumptuary laws, or statutes regulating how extravagantly people of the various social classes could dress, had been in effect for many years in England. Soon after taking the throne Elizabeth passed her own sumptuary acts, preserving the old standards and setting out in great detail what the different social ranks were allowed to wear.

By Elizabeth's acts, only royalty could wear the color purple and only the highest nobility could wear the color red. Ermine, a type of fur, was to be worn only by the royal family, gold could be worn only by nobles of the rank of earl or higher, and fur trims of any type were limited to people whose incomes were extremely high. The amount of detail in the sumptuary acts was remarkable, as can be seen in this excerpt from the act regarding women's clothing, as quoted on the *Elizabethan Era* Web site:

> None shall wear Any cloth of gold, tissue, nor fur of sables: except duchesses, marquises, and countesses in their gowns, kirtles [under-skirts], partlets [garments, usually made of lace, that filled the opening in the front of a dress and had a collar attached], and sleeves; cloth of gold, silver, tinseled satin, silk, or cloth mixed or embroidered with gold or silver or pearl, saving silk mixed with gold or silver in linings of cowls [a draped neckline], partlets, and sleeves: except all degrees above viscountesses, and viscountesses, baronesses, and other personages of like degrees in their kirtles and sleeves.

Elizabeth claimed the purpose of the sumptuary laws was to prohibit her subjects from wasting huge amounts of money on clothes. But the laws were also intended to preserve the existing order of social classes. As the incomes of the middle class increased, they were able to afford to live and dress like aristocrats. Thus it became increasingly important to regulate the garments of the various classes in order to maintain the established social order. The queen, as the highest-ranking person in the nation, was dressed the most elaborately, and she took this outward display of her position seriously. Although the punishment for wearing clothing prohibited by the sumptuary laws was a fine or worse, the laws were generally not enforced anywhere but in the royal court. However, purple and red dyes, velvet, gold cloth, and other forbidden garb were highly expensive, and poverty excluded the poor majority from wearing them. The poor, by necessity, dressed for their work: men wore boots, pants, a vest, shirt, and hat, while women wore an under skirt with an outer skirt over it, a bodice (the upper part of a woman's dress), shirt, and hat.

Young boys and girls alike were dressed in skirts until the age of about six. After that age children were dressed in smaller versions of adult clothing.

Food and drink

Wealthy English households usually ate large quantities of meat, such as beef, mutton (sheep), pork, venison (deer meat), and rabbit. Elizabethans tended to cook their meats with fruits, preferring the sweet taste. At social gatherings many varieties of meats and other foods were served. Because there were no refrigerators, meat was usually preserved in salt to last throughout the winter; the taste of old or spoiled meat was covered up with spices imported from Asia.

Meat was a rare luxury for the poorer classes. Their meals typically featured bread, eggs, and dairy products. Vegetables were also fairly rare in their diet.

Elizabethans rarely drank water because it was impure and could lead to sickness. Instead, people of all ages and classes drank wine, flat beer, or weak ale, even with their morning meal. Both classes ate bread, but not the same type. The wealthy usually ate a refined white wheat bread called manchet, while the poor were more likely to eat black or brown breads made from rye or barley.

Family

The nuclear family consisting only of a father, a mother, and their children made up the most common households in England, although very wealthy households sometimes included members of the extended family, such as aunts, uncles, cousins, and grandparents, and almost always included a large staff of live-in servants.

Among farm laborers and craftspeople, families were viewed as working units. Each member of the family had a task. On a farm, a young boy might be in charge of shooing birds away from the crops, an older boy might herd sheep, and the wife was in charge of maintaining the home, feeding the family, and helping her husband with raising and harvesting the crops. Girls usually were trained by their mothers to help take care of the household. Similarly, families in the cloth industry often worked in their homes and divided up the labor of spinning and weaving the cloth. For working people, it was a time-honored tradition that the son would take on the same career as his father.

There were few single people in Elizabethan England—all were expected to marry. In fact, women who did not marry were regarded with suspicion; some were even called witches. Married women were almost always homemakers, though poor women often had to work for pay as well. Almost all Elizabethans considered women to be inferior to

A wealthy Elizabethan family. GAMMA LIAISON NETWORK/GETTY IMAGES.

men. Except in special circumstances, women could not inherit the family property. They were expected to obey their male relatives and had few rights. It was equally expected that men would marry. Those who remained single had no legal claim as head of their household, and thus were not eligible for public office or to inherit from their families. Marriages were often arranged by parents. Most marriages were not made for romantic love, but for social or financial purposes. Divorce and separation were rare and required an act of Parliament. Only the very wealthy could even consider this option.

Almost all Elizabethan couples desired to have children. With a high mortality rate, or the frequency of deaths in proportion to a specific population, couples often had many children, knowing some would not survive. Generally, children were raised to be respectful and to serve their parents. They were viewed as the property of their fathers, and beatings and other severe punishments were a normal means of discipline in Elizabethan households. Parents' approaches to child rearing were very different from one another, however. Just as is the case today, some Elizabethan parents were prone to spoiling their children while others could be very strict.

Holidays and celebrations

England had a long and much beloved holiday tradition. For most Elizabethan workers, the workweek was long and hard; times for socializing and being entertained were eagerly anticipated. Many of the traditional English holidays were actually holy days, days honoring the lives of the saints (deceased people who, due to their exceptionally good behavior during life, receive the official blessing of the Catholic Church and are believed to be capable of interceding with God to protect people on earth) or events in the life of Jesus Christ. Holidays were celebrated within the parish, often with feasting and games as well as prayers.

The Reformation (the sixteenth-century religious movement that aimed to reform the Roman Catholic Church and resulted in the establishment of Protestant churches) brought about a change in the holidays celebrated in England and in the ways they were celebrated. The Anglican Church, the official Protestant church of England, and especially the Puritans (a group of Protestants who follow strict religious standards), wanted to eliminate the Catholic holidays, and they were far more rigid in their ideas of acceptable celebration behavior than the Catholic Church had been. In 1552 Elizabeth abolished most saints' days and issued an official Anglican list of the annual holy days.

Twelve Days of Christmas

One of the most popular holidays of the year was Christmas, which began on Christmas eve, December 24, and continued through January 6, the Twelfth Day (or Night). Christmas was preceded by a four-week period called Advent in which Elizabethans prayed and fasted, or refrained from eating certain foods at certain times. Advent ended with a Christmas Eve fast. On Christmas morning all attended a church service, and afterward the long fast was at last broken with a great feast. Celebrants went wassailing, going from house to house singing Christmas carols and enjoying a drink or treat at each stop. Music and other festivities continued for the next four days—all days off

A group of peasants celebrating Twelfth Night. © BETTMANN/CORBIS.

work. January 1, another work holiday, was the day of gift-giving. It was also celebrated with feasts and wassailing and other forms of merriment. The next and last Christmas holiday was the Twelfth Day or Night, also called Epiphany, which celebrated the arrival of the Three Magi, or wise men, at the manger of the infant Christ. The feast and revelries on the Twelfth Day were the most extravagant of the year.

Shrovetide

After Christmas, Shrovetide was the next major celebration. Shrovetide was the period consisting of the Sunday through the Tuesday before Ash Wednesday, the first day of Lent, or the forty-day period of fasting before Easter. Shrovetide celebrations included great feasts and many amusements; Shrovetide is the origin of the Mardi Gras celebrations that still take place today in many parts of the world.

May Day

The coming of summer was celebrated on May 1, also called May Day. Although it was officially a holiday in honor of two saints, Philip and Jacob, by custom it was mainly celebrated as a secular holiday. On the

Elizabethans dancing around a maypole in celebration of May Day. PUBLIC DOMAIN.

night before May Day, the youth of the village or town went out into the woods to gather mayflowers. The flowers were used to decorate houses, but most villages also used them to decorate a pole that the young men and women danced around the next day. The maypole dance is said to have involved kissing, and the Puritans worried that the holiday encouraged immoral behavior among the English youth. Although Elizabeth did not ban the traditional May Day celebrations, many local church leaders did. Still, it remained a popular holiday for many years to come.

Accession Day

Beginning on November 17, 1570, and continuing on that day annually, the English celebrated Queen Elizabeth's accession to the throne of England. Accession Day (also called Queen's Day) was one of the few entirely secular holidays of the year. The highlight of the day was the tilting tournaments performed in London for the queen, in which young nobles on horseback armed with lances, or long spears, charged at one another in an attempt to throw their opponent from his horse. Accession Day celebrated the queen's annual return to her London palaces for winter, and London became the site of great parades, music, dramatic presentations, and religious services dedicated to thanksgiving. Throughout England the day was celebrated with bonfires and the ringing of church bells. Though wealthy nobles had private celebrations, the Queen's Day was joyously celebrated among many working-class people. Throughout her reign Elizabeth had cultivated her image as the loving, and yet supremely regal, mother to her people—the Virgin Queen whose life was dedicated solely to caring for and protecting the English population. Though she had enemies among her subjects, Elizabeth was generally beloved and the holiday in her honor was a heartfelt celebration of the queen. The holiday was celebrated for nearly two hundred years after her death.

For More Information

BOOKS

Palliser, D. M. *The Age of Elizabeth: England Under the Later Tudors, 1547–1603.* 2d ed. London and New York: Longman, 1992.

Picard, Liza. *Elizabeth's London: Everyday Life in Elizabethan London.* New York: St. Martin's Press, 2003.

Wagner, John A. *Historical Dictionary of the Elizabethan World: Britain, Ireland, Europe, and America.* New York: Checkmark Books, 2002.

Wrightson, Keith. *English Society: 1580–1680.* New Brunswick, NJ: Rutgers University Press, 1982.

WEB SITES

Elizabethan Era. http://www.elizabethan-era.org.uk/elizabethan-clothing-laws-women.htm (accessed on July 11, 2006).

Monson, Shelly. *Elizabethan Holiday Customs.* http://guildofstgeorge.com/holiday.htm (accessed on July 11, 2006).

12

The Last Years of Elizabeth's Reign

The highest point of Queen Elizabeth I's (1533–1603; reigned 1558–1603) reign was the defeat of the Spanish Armada in 1588. (For more information on the Spanish Armada, see Chapter 7.) England could now lay claim to being the greatest sea power in the world. Most of those who still had lingering doubts about having a female leader fully embraced Elizabeth as their queen. But the defeat of the Armada did not signal smooth sailing ahead for Elizabeth. The war with Spain continued for fifteen more years. Other trials beset the aging queen in her last decade of life, including an increasing conflict with Ireland, several years of food shortage in England, and an uprising within her own court. Elizabeth's natural powers of leadership declined in her old age, and she suffered deep depressions, often set off by the deaths of her closest friends and advisors. Elizabeth's subjects began to lose confidence in their queen.

Conflict in Ireland

Elizabeth had inherited a complicated political situation in Ireland, an island lying just west of England. The country had been ruled by England, at least in name, since the twelfth century. At that time the Catholic pope, or head of the Roman Catholic Church, had declared the king of England to be the feudal lord of Ireland. (A feudal lord is the landowner and ruler of a district during the Middle Ages [c. 500–c. 1500] to whom the villagers owed loyalty, military service, and labor.) England maintained a loose control over Ireland, mainly leaving the operation of the government to the Irish lords and powerful families. In 1541, when Elizabeth's father, Henry VIII (1491–1547; reigned 1509–47), declared himself king of Ireland, he received the consent of the Irish Parliament.

Most of Ireland's population was concentrated in a wide area called the Pale that surrounded the city of Dublin. The Pale was ruled by lords who traced their ancestry back to the invading English of the twelfth century. Though their families had lived in Ireland for centuries these

WORDS TO KNOW

famine: The scarcity of food causing widespread hunger and starvation.

feudal lord: The landowner and ruler of a district during the Middle Ages (c. 500–c. 1500) to whom the villagers owed loyalty, military service, and labor.

malnutrition: Ill health caused by not eating enough food or not eating the proper balance of nutrients.

peasant: A class of farmers who worked in the fields owned by wealthy lords. Part of the crop was paid to the lord as rent.

Puritans: A group of Protestants who follow strict religious standards.

Reformation: A sixteenth century religious movement that aimed to reform the Roman Catholic Church and resulted in the establishment of Protestant churches.

theocracy: A state governed by religious, rather than political, principles.

---

lords considered themselves English and, up to a point, they were loyal to the English Crown. Notably, the remote northern Irish province of Ulster was outside the Pale and was not under English control.

The Reformation (the sixteenth-century religious movement that aimed to reform the Roman Catholic Church and resulted in the establishment of Protestant churches) created tension between Europe's Catholic and Protestant nations. Catholic countries, Spain in particular, believed that Protestant nations like England should be returned to Catholicism. Spain's King Philip II (1527–1598) realized that Ireland, whose people remained primarily Catholic, could be useful in an attack against England. England responded to this threat by tightening its control over the government in the Pale. This included attempts to convert the Irish to Protestantism.

In the early years of Elizabeth's reign English settlers were beginning to immigrate to Ireland. These early settlers viewed Ireland as an English colony. They taxed the Irish to maintain their English troops there. Resentment of English control resulted in Irish uprisings. Two unsuccessful Irish rebellions against England occurred in the early years of Elizabeth's reign. In the Desmond rebellion of 1579, the Irish were able to get help from some of the Catholic powers of Europe. England retaliated harshly, destroying fields and giving estates belonging to Irish lords to English nobles. Famine, a period when food is scarce, threatening

Irish rebel Hugh O'Neill.
HULTON ARCHIVE/GETTY
IMAGES.

a population with starvation, in Ireland resulted. Tens of thousands of people died and survivors faced terrible hardships.

As the years progressed England stationed more and more troops throughout Ireland, hoping to secure its own borders against a Spanish invasion. The Elizabethan government also attempted to expand its control into Ulster. The English treated the Irish with such contempt that even those lords who had traditionally remained loyal to England began to change their loyalties. In 1594 Ireland launched a large scale rebellion led by Hugh O'Neill (Earl of Tyrone; c. 1540–1616). This rebellion marked the start of what was known as the Nine Years' War (1594–1603).

Elizabeth responded by sending troops to put down O'Neill's rebellion. According to most historians Elizabeth made a large mistake in choosing the leadership for her Ireland campaign. In her last decades Elizabeth had continued to have favorites among the handsome young men of her court. Perhaps her strongest affection was given to the popular but temperamental and highly ambitious Robert Devereux (Earl of Essex; 1566–1601). Though Elizabeth doted on the young Devereux, she had little confidence in his abilities and had not placed him into the powerful positions he sought from her. In 1599, however, she placed him in command of a force of English soldiers on its way to stop the rebellion in Ireland. Devereux badly botched the mission. Instead of marching to Ulster to face O'Neill, he decided to first establish order in southern Ireland. He established garrisons, or military posts, throughout the region, assigning numerous troops there. His force suffered heavy casualties in the south, and his garrisoned soldiers suffered from unsanitary conditions and inadequate food. Thousands died from typhoid, dysentery, and other diseases. When he finally turned north, Devereux did not have enough troops to defeat O'Neill. He negotiated a truce. This was considered an extreme humiliation for England, and the queen was outraged. Devereux further complicated matters by leaving Ireland without Elizabeth's permission. The troublesome Nine Years' War continued, and did not end until one week after Elizabeth's death.

Famine

Elizabeth's reign had been marked by prosperity, but in 1594 the weather became abnormally wet and cold. For three years in a row England's crops failed. The peasant population was the first to suffer. (Peasants are farmers who worked in the fields owned by wealthy lords.) Since peasant farmers were required to pay a portion of their crop to the landowning lords as rent, they had only a small part of their crop to live on. When crops failed, peasants faced the very real threat of starvation. In desperation they killed their horses and oxen, used for plowing fields, for food. They also ate the seed intended for planting the next year. Once these sources were depleted peasants moved to the cities in search of food and employment.

People in cities also suffered as the price of grains and other resources rose steeply. The population had grown at a rapid rate and there were many more people to feed than in times past. In addition, the number of poor had risen dramatically as peasant farmers moved to the cities. Many of the poor suffered terribly from the lack of food. Only a small percentage died from actual starvation, at least in part because of poor laws that required local districts to aid the needy. (For more information on Elizabethan poor laws, see Chapter 11.) Nonetheless, there were thousands of deaths due to diseases related to malnutrition, or ill health caused by not eating enough food or not eating the proper balance of nutrients. By the late 1590s English systems of poor relief had become ineffective. Numerous uprisings broke out among the poor. Local authorities treated the rebel poor harshly, executing them in great numbers. Bitterness against the queen grew among the lower classes.

Betrayed by a favorite

When Devereux returned from Ireland, Elizabeth punished him severely for disobeying her instructions during the war. She banished him from court and denied him the positions and financial favors he had formerly enjoyed. Devereux was a hotheaded and extremely proud young man. He found it infuriating to be treated so harshly, particularly by a woman. He launched a poorly planned rebellion against the queen, enlisting young nobles who had their own conflicts with the queen. The small band of rebels rode into London, hoping to enlist the support of the townspeople. Although Devereux was popular in London, no one joined his uprising. Devereux was quickly arrested for treason. Elizabeth, in her late sixties, was forced to sign the death warrant of her favorite. Devereux was beheaded in 1601.

The last years

As the sixteenth century ended, the aging Elizabeth sank further into depression. As those closest to her died of old age, she became more isolated. Though she demanded to be treated as if she were still a young and attractive woman desired by all men, Elizabeth's former magnificence had faded. Her elaborate royal garments could not hide the evidence of time. She wore a red wig to cover her thinning hair and thick white powder to cover her wrinkles. No mirrors were allowed in

Elizabeth I on her deathbed. HULTON ARCHIVE/GETTY IMAGES.

court. In Elizabeth's last speech to Parliament in 1601, quoted in the United Kingdom Parliamentary Archives online, she acknowledged the great personal burden of being queen: "To be a King, and weare a Crown, is a thing more glorious to them that see it, then [than] it is pleasant to them that beare it."

In the winter of 1603 Elizabeth fell ill. Refusing medical treatment and food, she prepared herself for the end. She died in her bed in March. She was sixty-nine at the time of her death, and she had ruled England for forty-five years. James VI of Scotland (1566–1625) was proclaimed King James I of England a few hours after her death.

Elizabeth's legacy

Elizabeth strongly believed in the supremacy of the monarch as ruler. She had never believed in a representative government, viewing the rigid feudal social order, in which everyone knew their place, as the social order dictated by God. She believed that her power to rule England was absolute, granted by God, and thus beyond all human question. But Elizabeth was also well aware that she could only maintain power if she convinced her subjects that she was governing them well. She made sure that the people of England felt loved by their queen. She sought and often followed the advice of the most capable men in her kingdom. When necessary, she convened Parliament, England's legislative body, and surprised its members at times by listening carefully to their complaints and suggestions. Despite her own views about power Elizabeth granted the nobility and middle class a voice in her government, or at least the appearance of it. Thus under Elizabeth, the people of England were already heading toward a modern political system in which officials elected by the population ruled the country rather than monarchs who inherited their power. But the path to English democracy would be a rocky one.

Perhaps Elizabeth's most far-reaching policies were her moderate views toward the national religion. When all of Europe was deeply divided after the Reformation, the queen was careful to bring together the moderate English Catholics and Puritans within her government and council. Elizabeth brought an impressive amount of unity to a country that might otherwise have erupted into opposing factions. This unity did not survive the queen for very long.

The kings that followed Elizabeth tried to restrict the powers of the Parliament, which had become largely Puritan, and in 1642 civil war broke out in England. This was a series of political and armed conflicts

James VI of Scotland succeeded Elizabeth. © BETTMANN/ CORBIS.

between those who favored a representative government led by Parliament and those who supported the supreme rule of a monarch. In1649 Puritan parliamentary leader Oliver Cromwell (1599–1658) took control of England, abolishing both the monarchy and Parliament. After his death

Some Famous Film Portrayals of Elizabeth I

Elizabeth has been a popular subject of numerous films over the years. Some of the most famous movies, along with the actresses who played Elizabeth, are listed below:

1912: *Queen Elizabeth,* starring Sarah Bernhardt (silent).

1923: *The Virgin Queen,* starring Diana Manners (silent).

1937: *Fire Over England,* starring Flora Robson as the queen.

1939: *The Private Lives of Essex and Elizabeth,* starring Bette Davis.

1955: *The Virgin Queen,* starring Bette Davis in her second portrayal of Elizabeth.

1968: *Elizabeth the Queen,* starring Judith Anderson.

1971: *Elizabeth R,* starring Glenda Jackson (six-part series for television).

1971: *Mary Queen of Scots,* starring Glenda Jackson in her second portrayal of Elizabeth.

1998: *Elizabeth,* starring Cate Blanchett.

1998: *Shakespeare in Love,* featuring Judi Dench as Elizabeth.

2006: *Elizabeth I: Parts One and Two* starring Helen Mirren (two-part series for television).

the English reestablished the monarchy under Charles II (1630–1685). This was called the Restoration of 1660. But by this time it clear that the king of England no longer held absolute power, and Charles worked with Parliament to rule the nation. His successor, James II (1633–1701), though, was a Catholic who refused to share power. The English population was unwilling to be torn apart by each succeeding monarch. In 1688 when the king's son-in-law, William III (1650–1702), led a rebellion against the king called the Glorious Revolution. William and his wife, Mary II (1662–1694), took over the English throne, but they consented to a constitution that forever limited the authority of the English monarchy. Elizabeth I would have mourned this act as a violation of the proper order of society, and yet many historians credit her with helping to bring about a more democratic society.

After the death of Elizabeth, the image of the queen that had been promoted throughout her lifetime—the embodiment of national pride in England and the golden age in its cultural life—came to be revered. Many historians believe that the image of the strong, loving, self-sacrificing Virgin Queen was simply Elizabeth's creation and had little to do with the real-life headstrong, vain, and temperamental queen. Others point to the stability and strength England acquired during Elizabeth's reign, a time when its rival, France, crumbled due to the religious wars between

Catholics and Protestants. Many give Elizabeth at least some of the credit for England's golden age. The fascination with the Virgin Queen has never dwindled. Elizabeth has remained an extremely popular subject for biographers and historians, as well as novelists and filmmakers.

For More Information

BOOKS

Brigden, Susan. *New Worlds, Lost Worlds: The Rule of the Tudors, 1485–1603.* New York: Penguin, 2000.

Schama, Simon. *A History of Britain: At the Edge of the World? 3500 BC –1603 AD.* New York: Hyperion, 2000.

Smith, Lacey Baldwin. *The Elizabethan Epic.* London: Panther Books, 1966.

Weir, Alison. *The Life of Elizabeth I.* New York: Ballantine Books,1998.

WEB SITES

"Death of Queen Elizabeth." United Kingdom Parliamentary Archives. http://www.parliament.uk/parliamentary_publications_and_archives/parliamentary_archives/archives___elizabeth_i.cfm (accessed on July 11, 2006).

"Famine." *Bvio.com.* http://bvio.ngic.re.kr/Bvio/index.php/Famine (accessed on July 11, 2006).

"The Original Elizabeth: Here's a List of Movies about the English Queen to Rent or Buy." *Newsweek,* exclusively for MSNBC on the web. April 16, 2006. http://www.msnbc.msn.com/id/12331339/site/newsweek/ (accessed July 11, 2006).

Pilib de Longbhuel, Máirtán. "Nine Years' War." *Ireland's OWN History.* http://irelandsown.net/9years.html (accessed on July 11, 2006).

Where to Learn More

Books

Bernard, G. W. *The King's Reformation: Henry VIII and the Remaking of the English Church.* New Haven, CT and London: Yale University Press, 2005.

Brigden, Susan. *New Worlds, Lost Worlds: The Rule of the Tudors, 1485–1603.* New York: Penguin Books, 2000.

Brimacombe, Peter. *All the Queen's Men: The World of Elizabeth I.* New York: St. Martin's Press, 2000.

Bryant, Arthur. *The Elizabethan Deliverance.* New York: St. Martin's Press, 1981.

Dersin, Denise, ed.*What Life Was Like in the Realm of Elizabeth: England A.D. 1533–1603.* Alexandria, VA: Time-Warner Books, 1998.

Doran, Susan. *Queen Elizabeth I.* New York: New York University Press, 2003.

Dunn, Jane. *Elizabeth and Mary: Cousins, Rivals, Queens.* New York: Alfred A. Knopf, 2004.

Greenblatt, Stephen. *Will in the World: How Shakespeare Became Shakespeare.* New York: Norton, 2004.

Gregory, Brad S. *Salvation at Stake: Christian Martyrdom in Early Modern Europe.* Cambridge, MA and London, UK: Harvard University Press, 1999.

Hanson, Neil. *The Confident Hope of a Miracle: The True History of the Spanish Armada.* New York: Knopf, 2005.

Kirkpatrick, Robin. *The European Renaissance, 1400–1600.* Harlow, England: Pearson Education, 2002.

Martin, Colin and Geoffrey Parker. *The Spanish Armada.* New York: Norton, 1988.

Miller, Helen Hill. *Captains from Devon: The Great Elizabethan Seafarers Who Won the Oceans for England.* Chapel Hill, NC: Algonquin Books, 1985.

Morrill, John, ed. *The Oxford Illustrated History of Tudor & Stuart Britain.* Oxford, England and New York: Oxford University Press, 1996.

Orme, Nicholas. *Medieval Schools: From Roman Britain to Tudor England.* New Haven, CT and London, England: Yale University Press, 2006.

Palliser, D. M. *The Age of Elizabeth: England Under the Later Tudors, 1547–1603,* 2d ed. London and New York: Longman, 1992.

Picard, Liza. *Elizabeth's London: Everyday Life in Elizabethan London.* New York: St. Martin's Press, 2003.

Powicke, Sir Maurice. *The Reformation in England.* London: Oxford University Press, 1941.

Ridley, Jasper. *Bloody Mary's Martyrs: The Story of England's Terror.* New York: Carroll & Graf Publishers, 2001.

Rollins, Hyder E. and Herschel Baker, eds. *The Renaissance in England.* Boston: D. C. Heath and Company, 1954.

Rowse, A. L. *Eminent Elizabethans.* Athens: University of Georgia Press, 1983.

———. *The England of Elizabeth: The Structure of Society.* New York: Macmillan, 1961.

Ruoff, James E. *Major Elizabethan Poetry & Prose.* New York: Thomas Y. Crowell Company, 1972.

Schama, Simon. *A History of Britain: At the Edge of the World? 3500 BC–1603 AD.* New York: Hyperion, 2000.

Singman, Jeffrey L. *Daily Life in Elizabethan England.* Westport, CT and London, England: Greenwood Press, 1995.

Starkey, David. *Elizabeth: The Struggle for the Throne.* New York: Perennial, 2001.

Strachey, Lytton. *Elizabeth and Essex: A Tragic History.* Harvest Books, 2002.

Thomas, Jane Resh. *Behind the Mask: The Life of Queen Elizabeth I.* Boston, MA: Clarion Books, Houghton Mifflin, 1998.

Tillyard, E. M. W. *The Elizabethan World Picture.* New York: Vintage Books, 1942.

Watkins, Susan, with photographs by Mark Fiennes. *In Public and in Private: Elizabeth I and Her World.* London: Thames and Hudson, 1998.

Weir, Alison *The Life of Elizabeth I.* New York: Ballantine Books, 1998.

Wells, Stanley. *Shakespeare for All Time.* Oxford, England and New York: Oxford University Press, 2003.

Wightman, W. P. D. *Science in a Renaissance Society.* London: Hutchinson University Library, 1972.

Wood, Michael. *Shakespeare.* New York: Basic Books, 2003.

Web Sites

BBC: Historic Figures. http://www.bbc.co.uk/history/historic_figures/ (accessed on July 11, 2006).

BBC History. http://www.bbc.co.uk/history/ (accessed on July 11, 2006).

Catholic Encyclopedia, http://www.newadvent.org/cathen/index.html (accessed on July 11, 2006).

Classic Literature Library: British Authors. http://www.classic-literature.co.uk/ british-authors/ (accessed on July 11, 2006).

Educating Shakespeare. http://www.likesnail.org.uk/welcome-es.htm (accessed on July 24, 2006).

Elizabeth I. http://www.elizabethi.org/ (accessed on July 24, 2006).

Elizabeth's Pirates. http://www.channel4.com/history/microsites/H/history/ pirates/ (accessed on July 11, 2006).

Elizabethan Authors. http://www.elizabethanauthors.com (accessed on July 11, 2006).

Elizabethan Costume Page. http://www.elizabethancostume.net (accessed on July 24, 2006).

Elizabethan Era. http://www.elizabethan-era.org.uk/ (accessed on July 11, 2006).

Elizabethan Holiday Customs. http://guildofstgeorge.com/holiday.htm (accessed on July 11, 2006).

Elizabethan Law Overview. http://www.twingroves.district96.k12.il.us/ Renaissance/Courthouse/ElizaLaw.html (accessed on July 24, 2006).

English Bible History. http://www.greatsite.com/timeline-english-bible-history/ (accessed on July 11, 2006).

History of the British Monarchy. http://www.royal.gov.uk/output/Page1.asp (accessed on July 24, 2006).

In Search of Shakespeare. http://www.pbs.org/shakespeare/ (accessed on July 11, 2006).

The Marlowe Society. http://www.marlowe-society.org/ (accessed on July 11, 2006).

Mary, Queen of Scots. http://www.marie-stuart.co.uk/ (accessed on July 11, 2006).

Medieval History. http://www.medievalhistory.net (accessed on July 11, 2006).

Renaissance Central. http://www.rencentral.com (accessed on July 11, 2006).

Sir Francis Drake: A Pictorial Biography. Published in Amsterdam by N. Israel, 1970. Copyright © 1970 by H. P. Kraus. Library of Congress: Rare Books and Special Collections Reading Room. http://www.loc.gov/rr/rarebook/ catalog/drake/ (accessed on July 11, 2006).

16th Century Renaissance English Literature. http://www.luminarium.org/renlit/ (accessed on July 11, 2006).

Shakespeare Homepage. http://www.shakespeare.org.uk/content/view/10/10/ (accessed on July 11, 2006).

Shakespeare's Life and Times. Internet Shakespeare Editions, University of Victoria: Victoria, BC, 2001–2005. http://ise.uvic.ca/Library/SLT/intro/introcite.html (accessed on July 11, 2006).

Shakespeare Online. http://www.shakespeare-online.com/index.html (accessed on July 11, 2006).

Shakespeare Resource Center. http://www.bardweb.net/ (accessed on July 11, 2006).

Sonnet Central. http://www.sonnets.org/eliz.htm (accessed on July 11, 2006).

Tudor England: 1485 to 1603. http://englishhistory.net/tudor.html (accessed on July 11, 2006).

Tudor History. http://tudorhistory.org (accessed on July 24, 2006).

Tudor Place. http://www.tudorplace.com.ar/ (accessed on July 11, 2006).

Index

Illustrations are marked by (ill.).